# HUNGRY

## FOR HARBOR COUNTRY

# HUNGRY

## FOR HARBOR COUNTRY®

RECIPES AND STORIES *from*
THE COAST OF SOUTHWEST MICHIGAN

## LINDSAY NAVAMA

PHOTOGRAPHY BY GABRIELLE SUKICH

MIDWAY

AN AGATE IMPRINT

CHICAGO

10 9 8 7 6 5 4 3 2 1      20 21 22 23 24 25

ISBN-13: 978-1-57284-287-8
ISBN-10: 1-57284-287-3
eISBN-13: 978-1-57284-838-2
eISBN-10: 1-57284-838-3

Cover and interior design by Morgan Krehbiel
Cover photo by Gabrielle Sukich
Cover styled by Emily Anstadt
Author photo by Gabrielle Sukich

Library of Congress Cataloging-in-Publication Data

Names: Navama, Lindsay, author. | Sukich, Gabrielle, photographer.
Title: Hungry for Harbor Country : Recipes and stories from the coast of Southwest Michigan / Lindsay Navama ; photography by Gabrielle Sukich.
Description: Chicago : Midway, an Agate Imprint, 2020. | Includes index. |
   Summary: "Escape to Harbor Country with 56 lake-life recipes and stories
   that capture the celebratory spirit of this Michigan vacation
   destination"-- Provided by publisher.
Identifiers: LCCN 2019043781 | ISBN 9781572842878 (hardcover)
Subjects: LCSH: Cooking, American--Midwestern style. | Cooking (Natural
   Foods) | Cooking--Michigan--New Buffalo. | Navama, Lindsay--Homes and
   haunts. | LCGFT: Cookbooks.
Classification: LCC TX715.2.M53 N38 2020 | DDC 641.5977⁴⁄1--dc23
LC record available at https://lccn.loc.gov/2019043781

Midway Books is an imprint of Agate Publishing. Agate books are available in bulk at discount prices. For more information, visit agatepublishing.com.

# Dedication

To my mom and dad, for letting me be your third wheel at most restaurants growing up and for giving me the courage to try everything at least once, from unforgettable moo shu pork and sashimi to albóndigas soup and fondue. I'm forever grateful I was born into a family who "lives to eat!" Thanks to your endless love and support, I dare to dream.

Mom, you taught me from an early age how to "host with the most," and that we could recreate some of our most memorable restaurant meals right at home in our Tahoe kitchen, without a recipe!

Dad, thanks for passing on your "seasoning gene" and always being willing to try whatever interesting concoctions I made from ages 5 to 12, when I was deep in my "exploratory" phase as a young home chef.

To David, my husband and soul match, for waking up one winter Saturday and deciding we should day trip to Michigan. Camp Navama was born out of your relentless quest to find us a (non-temporary) place, away from the noise, where our minds could be quiet, our hearts full, and our souls at peace. This book would not exist without your boundless dedication to our love. Thank you for choosing me in this life. You are my forever adventure.

# Contents

# Introduction

I GREW UP IN Tahoe City, a tiny lake town with one stoplight. Like so many small-town kids, I couldn't wait to escape rural life and move to the big city. For me, that city was L.A., then Chicago when my husband, David, and I moved there for work.

On one morning in Chicago, my husband woke up and he was hungry. But he wasn't craving his usual weekend breakfast request of gluten-free, dairy-free blueberry chocolate chip pancakes. He was hungry for an adventure away from the crowds and concrete of the city. Within hours we were in a Zipcar, speeding away from Chicago toward Harbor Country, Michigan, which according to friends, promised rural towns, country roads, u-pick farms, and a generous slice of quiet.

That first day trip took us around the southern curve of Lake Michigan, through many beachside hamlets, to the artsy town of Saugatuck. Two hundred eighty miles and numerous delicious local treats later, we arrived back in Chicago. Our simple Saturday morning hunger for a rural escape had grown into a ravenous appetite to create a space where we could stress a bit less and live a lot more.

We continued to make visits to Harbor Country, and on one of our many trips, we drove by a sign reading "Harbor Country: A Place to Be Yourself." The words on that billboard remained at the top of my mind as we began a house hunt in the area, with the goal of finding more permanent peace.

At that time I had very much lost myself. David and I had spent the past three years in Chicago trying to make the Midwest city feel like home after being bound to the West Coast since birth. And to ice that cake, I was also searching for my next career.

The truth is, I had never pictured living anywhere but California, and since leaving Tahoe, I had zero interest in returning to a small town. But the more we explored New Buffalo and the surrounding Harbor Country region, I was reminded for the first time in a long time of the many things I actually loved about growing up in the rural High Sierra mountains. When it comes to early morning beach walks, afternoon hikes, invigorating sunset swims, beach bonfires, knowing your neighbors, and falling asleep to the sound of silence, the city just can't compete.

Late that spring, we finally settled on a little nugget of a home in New Buffalo, just 90 minutes from the city. We took a breath—not a shallow, breathing-to-get-by kind of breath. A long, strong inhale that clears a frenzied mind, calms a pounding heart, and restores the peace within.

As we relaxed into the warmth and community of our first Harbor Country summer, we felt our spirits unfurl and reconnect to life's most delicious pleasures. We weren't sure what to expect from the months ahead, but for the first time in a long time, we were both really hungry! Hungry to host friends and family, excited to savor more sunsets, and committed to taking bigger, juicier bites out of every single lake-life moment. After spending a single summer at "Camp Navama," our New Buffalo home, I discovered this was not only a place to be yourself, but a place to find yourself.

I returned to my happiest place—the kitchen—and began cooking with heart again. I cooked for David, for family, and for friends new and old, revisiting forgotten recipes from my days as a recipe developer, private chef, and owner of Cookies Couture, a boutique bakery. I spent hours perfecting gluten-free and cow dairy–free versions of my hubby's favorite foods and filled our table with dishes made from the incredible variety of produce farmed here in Berrien County. Friendships were forged with local farmers, chefs, restaurant proprietors, artisans, and makers who all spent their days feeding this community.

Our first 52 weeks at Camp Navama were so *unexpectedly delicious* that I wanted to capture each magical moment and preserve them in mason jars to enjoy endlessly. As a food-loving family, many of our best memories that year centered on meals shared around our New Buffalo table. I soaked up the whimsical energy of Harbor Country, which allowed me to cook like one only can when the days feel endless and the heart is wide open.

While memories sadly can't be preserved in glass jars like summer's bounty, recipes allow us to relive treasured moments in time. At Camp Navama, week after week, month after month, we continued making food to feed our friends and souls and to honor the changing seasons. This cooking marathon left me with a vibrant collection of recipes and stories—a paper trail of how we celebrated our first year in Harbor Country.

Memorable meals and unforgettable people inspired this cookbook, organized by our seasonal rituals. When it wasn't time to host, it was time to hammock, or build a fire, or pack a picnic and raise a glass for sunset hour, then indulge in a deliciously sweet treat before falling asleep to the sound of silence.

The recipes here are meant to please many palates. While living in L.A., we often hosted dinner parties with a few gluten-free guests, three vegans, the token pescatarian, and our friends who don't eat pork. Today, no matter what coast I'm cooking on, I see many people who struggle with food sensitivities or simply have developed specific food preferences. Whatever your pleasure, I've got you covered with options for using gluten-free flour *or* regular all-purpose flour and dairy-free milk *or* your milk of choice. Want to start your day with a marshmallow-topped café au lait, enjoy kale salad midday, then indulge in brisket and birthday cake at night? Me too! We're on the same page, friends.

If years ago someone had told me I'd be living in the Midwest, in a tiny town no less, I would have known with utter certainty that they were mistaken—that they had the wrong girl. Today I'm beyond grateful that life doesn't always unravel as planned. Around any given corner you may very well find something unexpectedly delicious.

P.S. If you have any questions about a recipe, you can probably find me at David's, Infusco, or Whistle Stop on any given weekend—or feel free to connect through my blog at ThirdCoastKitchen.com.

# How to Use This Book

Here is your inside guide to quickly and easily understand how to use this book and know what ingredients you'll want to have on hand to whip up many of these recipes at a moment's notice. After all, lake life is a little more free-form and a little less planned, and that's what makes it so delicious! Because I want to help you feed *all* friends and family, my recipes are easily adapted for people *with* and *without* food sensitivities. In most recipes I offer alternate options, such as "gluten-free flour" *or* "regular all-purpose flour" and "almond milk" *or* "milk of choice."

### A Note on Time Zones

Please note that Harbor Country is located very close to a time zone boundary. Most places listed in this book operate on eastern time, though some places in Indiana operate on central time. If you're visiting from Chicago or elsewhere, please keep this in mind when planning your trip.

# Before You Go Forth to Cook with Wild Abandon . . . Know This

**Read It All**  Reading the recipe from start to end is well worth the few minutes it takes.

**Mise en Place**  A mise en place is your best friend in the kitchen. Pronounced "meez ahn plas," this is a French term meaning "set in place." Creating your mise en place means taking time to set out, cut, prepare, and measure all ingredients before cooking. If a recipe calls for 2 cups pitted cherries, you'll want to pit those before you begin cooking. A mise en place is helpful for any recipe, but especially those with more ingredients and steps. It also prevents you from getting halfway through the recipe and realizing you are out of an ingredient!

**Flour Substitutions**  My recipes use gluten-free flour by default. Want to use regular flour? No problem! Unless otherwise noted, you can substitute regular all-purpose flour for the gluten-free flour called for in any recipe (excluding the recipes in the Secret Local Recipes chapter).

**Dairy Substitutions**  My recipes use salted butter and almond milk by default. Unless otherwise noted, you can substitute vegan butter for salted butter and your milk of choice for almond milk in any recipe (excluding the recipes in the Secret Local Recipes chapter).

**Secret Local Recipes**  The recipes in the Secret Local Recipes chapter were contributed by local chefs and friends. While some are naturally gluten- or dairy-free, others are not. I did not alter these with substitutions, as they are presented in this book exactly the way the contributors intended.

**Oven Rack Positions**  Unless otherwise noted in the directions, your oven rack should be in the middle position.

# Sidebars and Helpful Tips

**Map Sidebars**  Throughout the book, I highlight some of my favorite farms, restaurants, coffee shops, and more and reference where they are in Harbor Country. There is also a full list of all the locations I mention in the book (plus more!) on page 225.

**Special Items Needed**  This heading, which can be found above certain items in the ingredients list, denotes any tools used in the recipe that some people may not normally have in the kitchen (especially in a vacation home), making it easy to plan ahead and pick up anything you're missing before cooking begins. You may notice some items—like heavy-duty aluminum foil—are listed as special items in certain recipes but not in others. I only include items in this section if they are absolutely essential to make the recipe.

**Tips for Success**  These sidebars highlight *important directions* or helpful tips and tricks throughout the book, such as bringing eggs to room temperature quickly by placing them in a small bowl of warm water for about 5 minutes.

**Freestyle**  Life at the lake tends to flow a little more freely, and in my kitchen, I aim to inspire people to take a playful, creative approach to cooking. This means learning to use recipes as a road map but knowing when it's totally okay to stray from the trail. "Freestyle" sidebars invite you to explore and choose slightly different preparation methods, ingredients, or seasoning options, depending on your needs and preferences. Just because I like my café au lait (page 158) with vanilla doesn't mean you can't try yours with that locally made lavender syrup you just picked up at the farmers market!

# My Harbor Country Pantry

My Kitchen Mantra: I aim to feed myself, family, and friends with whole, unprocessed foods that taste delicious, are nutritious, and make you glow from the inside out. Occasionally frosting, white chocolate, or sugar cereal makes a kitchen cameo, and that's okay—as long as whole foods are the star of the show!

In addition to your basic pantry items, here is a list of other ingredients I keep stocked that allow me to cook with healthier whole foods, adapt easily to food allergies when necessary, and let my freestyle flag fly when I want to get more creative in the kitchen!

**Unless Otherwise Noted, in Recipes I'm Using** Organic produce; organic large eggs; organic salted butter; grapeseed, coconut, avocado, or olive oil; unsweetened almond milk; organic coconut sugar; organic agave, organic evaporated cane juice; kosher or fine sea salt; fresh ground black pepper.

**About Gluten-Free Flour** Many brands now offer "all-purpose" gluten-free flour blends. *Some contain xanthan gum and some do not.* In recipes calling for gluten-free flour, I specify whether you need to use a version *with* or *without* xanthan gum. Using the correct version is important for a successful outcome because xanthan gum can change how the flour "gets along" with the other ingredients. Blends containing xanthan gum can typically replace regular all-purpose flour at a 1:1 ratio.

## Flours, Oats, and Meals

All-purpose gluten-free flour *with* xanthan gum: I use Cup4Cup Multipurpose Flour, King Arthur Measure for Measure Flour, or Bob's Red Mill 1 to 1 Baking Flour.

All-purpose gluten-free flour *without* xanthan gum: I use King Arthur All-Purpose Gluten-Free Flour or Bob's Red Mill Gluten Free All-Purpose Baking Flour.

Regular all-purpose flour: If you don't have a gluten sensitivity, lucky you! In my recipes calling for gluten-free flour, feel free to replace it with your choice of regular all-purpose flour. I love King Arthur brand.

Almond flour: Cannot be replaced with regular all-purpose flour or gluten-free flour.

Coconut flour: Cannot be replaced with regular all-purpose flour or gluten-free flour.

Buckwheat flour: Cannot be replaced with regular all-purpose flour or gluten-free flour.

Cornmeal

Old-fashioned rolled oats: Gluten-free or regular varieties can be used in all recipes.

## Sweeteners

Honey

Maple syrup

Agave

Coconut sugar

Brown sugar

Organic evaporated cane juice

## Seasonings

Kosher salt

Sea salt

Freshly ground black pepper

Ground white pepper

Red pepper flakes

Ground turmeric

Ground cinnamon

Ground ginger

Ground nutmeg

Pure vanilla extract

## Milks, Cheeses, Butter, Oils, and Eggs

Unsweetened almond milk: I use Elmhurst, Almond Breeze, or Califia Farms.

Unsweetened oat milk: I use Elmhurst or Oatly.

Cans of full-fat coconut milk

Goat milk or sheep milk cheese

Coconut oil

Avocado oil

Olive oil

Organic large eggs

Salted butter: Many baking recipes call for unsalted butter. I prefer to use salted butter in most cases, as salty-sweet flavors really excite the taste buds, but feel free to use unsalted butter if you prefer.

## Produce

Lemons

Limes

Red onions

Shallots

Fresh herbs: I often use basil, thyme, rosemary, mint, sage, and dill.

## Local Harbor Country Products

Part of what made us love Harbor Country was witnessing how the community supports local businesses. I buy the following ingredients locally whenever possible: honey, maple syrup, jam, produce (cherries, berries, apples, peaches, plums, grapes, asparagus, corn, tomatoes, squash, zucchini, and pumpkins), chicken, seafood, meat, eggs (duck and chicken), cheese, coffee, and spirits.

# Impress Your Guests

I N THIS CHAPTER, I'm sharing eight of my favorite lake-life dishes that you can always rely on to be the star of the party and impress your guests. Each delivers surprise and delight, while unexpected flavor combinations and unique preparation methods pique culinary curiosities.

Growing up, my mom was stellar at planning the perfect dinner party. Early on, she taught me the "KIS method" for menu planning: *keep it simple!* That means choosing one impressive recipe that might be a bit more time-consuming, then filling in the table with deliciously simple dishes that let the ingredients shine. That way, you can relax while cooking for a crowd!

These are some of the recipes our guests enjoyed most during our first year at Camp Navama. Inspired by Southwest Michigan's bountiful local produce and the passionate food artisans in Harbor Country, these dishes use ingredients from some of my go-to places for top-quality meat, seafood, fruits, and vegetables, including Dinges' Fall Harvest, Flagship Specialty Foods and Fish Market, Kaminski Farms, and Springhope Farm.

The next time you host a party, consciously relish the moment and honor the time you've carved out to prepare beautiful food for the wonderful people in your life.

# I Am Grapeful

**M**Y HUSBAND, DAVID, and I discovered **Dinges' Fall Harvest** one bluebird-sky morning when we were biking through the countryside. Intrigued by the craft barn filled with dried gourds for sale, we stopped for a closer look. Our gourd shopping was interrupted by several loud squawks coming from behind the barn. We got ready to flee, but then farmer Lee Dinges rode up on his tractor, introduced himself, and invited us to take a peek at the birds his grandkids were taking to the county fair.

Around the back of the barn, our citified souls were greeted by exotic birds, chickens, bunnies, and white turkeys (one of which eventually ended up coming home with us for our first true "farm to table" Thanksgiving). Meals become extra special when you meet the farmer who cares for the land that feeds your family. We thanked Lee for the feathered friend tour and promised to come back in the fall when his property became a pumpkin patch and his grapes were ready to harvest.

That September, we visited the farm just before sunset, filling far too many bags with deep blue Concord grapes and golden, sun-kissed Niagaras the color of chardonnay. My mind began reeling with recipe ideas, because a girl can only eat so many grapes straight off the vine.

The Crisp Chicken with Roasted Grapes and Brown Butter Grape Sauce is one of many grape-forward meals I made that fall, and if you've never roasted grapes, my friend, your life is about to get really juicy!

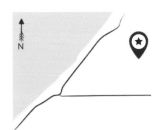

★ Dinges' Fall Harvest

15219 Mill Rd. | Three Oaks, MI

As the leaves turn and days become crisp, many families take a trip to Dinges' Fall Harvest. Every year, the pumpkin patch brims with orange and white globes in all sizes and varieties imaginable, and a massive cornfield maze and spooky decorations deliver a world of Halloween happiness.

# Crisp Chicken with Roasted Grapes and Brown Butter Grape Sauce

¶¶ **4–6** succulent servings    ⏱ **45 min** active time    ⧖ **9 hrs 30 min** start to finish

SPECIAL ITEMS NEEDED

Fine mesh strainer or food mill

CRISP CHICKEN

8–10 organic chicken thighs, bone-in, skin-on

Kosher salt and freshly ground black pepper, to taste

2 pounds seedless grapes, stemmed, for roasting (Use a mix of green and red or black grapes for a pretty plate!)

2 tablespoons olive oil, plus more as needed

BROWN BUTTER GRAPE SAUCE

2 pounds Concord grapes, stemmed (Use Dinges' Concord grapes in the fall or buy red grapes in a pinch. Buy Concord grape juice if you're short on time.)

¾ cup salted butter, cut into 1-inch cubes

2 tablespoons stemmed and minced fresh thyme, plus more for garnish

2 teaspoons white wine vinegar

¼ cup cold water

1½ tablespoons cornstarch

Kosher salt and freshly ground black pepper, to taste

**Dry Out the Chicken Skin**  Place the thighs skin side up in a single layer on a baking sheet. Pat dry with a paper towel. Refrigerate, uncovered, for 6 to 8 hours or overnight to dry the skin.

**Preheat the Oven**  Align a rack in the center of the oven and another rack just below it, and then preheat the oven to 425°F (on the roast setting, if you have one).

**Prepare the Chicken**  Remove the chicken from the refrigerator and let rest at room temperature for 30 minutes. Place on a plate and sprinkle both sides of each chicken thigh with salt and pepper. Then place the chicken thighs, *skin side up*, in the center of a large cast iron skillet or oven-safe skillet.

**Roast the Chicken**  Place the chicken on the center oven rack and roast for about 20 minutes.

**Prepare the Grapes**  While the chicken is roasting, line a baking sheet with aluminum foil, then brush it with oil. Place the seedless grapes in a single layer on the prepared baking sheet. Drizzle with about 2 tablespoons of the olive oil and toss to coat. Sprinkle with pepper.

**Roast the Grapes**  Place the seedless grapes in the oven on the rack just below the chicken and roast both for 20 to 25 more minutes, until the grape skins begin to blister and the internal temperature of the chicken reaches 165°F.

**Juice the Concord Grapes**  While the seedless grapes and chicken roast, start the sauce. Place the Concord grapes in a blender and blend 1 to 2 minutes on high speed. Press the juice through a fine mesh strainer or food mill to strain the juice from the skins. Set the juice aside and discard the skins.

**Prepare the Brown Butter Grape Sauce**  In a medium saucepan, melt the butter over medium-high heat, whisking often, until it foams and just begins to brown. Reduce the heat to a low simmer. Watch carefully. Add the Concord grape juice to the saucepan and whisk to combine. Add the thyme and vinegar and simmer on medium-low heat for 12 to 15 minutes, until the sauce begins to reduce.

In a small bowl, whisk together the cold water and cornstarch until smooth in order to make a slurry. Add the slurry to the pan and raise the heat to bring the sauce to a strong simmer, whisking constantly for about 5 minutes, or until the sauce thickens enough to coat the back of a spoon. Whisk in salt and pepper to taste, then simmer for another 3 to 5 minutes. Remove from the heat and set aside.

**Let's Eat!**  To serve family style, tuck some of the roasted grapes around the chicken in the skillet. Place the remaining roasted grapes in a bowl and serve the grape sauce in a gravy boat.

For individual portions, pour ½ cup of the grape sauce in the center of each plate. Place 1 to 2 chicken thighs on top of the sauce, skin side up. Surround the chicken with ¾ cup roasted grapes, sprinkle with fresh thyme, and drizzle about 2 tablespoons grape sauce on top of the chicken.

# Shrimp, Scallops, and Squid, Oh My!

M Y HUSBAND LOVES seafood pasta, and mine used to be his favorite until I was shown up royally one summer evening in the coastal village of Levanto, Italy. At dinner one night, he ordered homemade gluten-free seafood pasta. (Italy offers incredible gluten-free foods.) It arrived baked in a steaming parchment paper parcel and strewn with garlic, San Marzano tomatoes, plump prawns, tender baby octopus, white rings of calamari, and buttery scallops. As he ate, his eyes glistened, and it wasn't because of the house Chianti. At that moment I knew this dish was going to follow us home.

We celebrated our first wedding anniversary at Camp Navama in early June of 2017, and because food is my love language, I recreated the parchment paper–baked pasta that had won his heart.

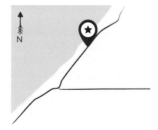

★ Flagship Specialty Foods and
Fish Market

14939 Red Arrow Hwy. | Lakeside, MI

Thanks to the fresh seafood locally available at Flagship Specialty Foods and Fish Market and a bottle of Chianti from our wedding weekend, I successfully unpacked the taste memory from Levanto right in my New Buffalo kitchen.

# Third Coast Seafood Pasta Baked in Parchment

🍴 **6–8** sea-loving servings  ⧗ **1 hr** start to finish

SPECIAL ITEMS NEEDED

Parchment paper or heavy-duty aluminum foil

---

1 tablespoon plus 2 teaspoons kosher salt, divided

⅓ cup plus 1 tablespoon olive oil, divided, plus more as needed

10 ounces small to medium calamari, cleaned and cut into rings if whole

12 large dry sea scallops cut into quarters, or 30 fresh dry bay scallops (see Tips for Success)

¾ pound fresh or thawed frozen shrimp, peeled, cleaned, and deveined

4 large cloves garlic, peeled and chopped

1 (28-ounce) can whole Italian plum tomatoes (I love San Marzano.)

2 cups cherry tomatoes, halved

½ cup stemmed and finely chopped fresh Italian parsley

½ teaspoon red pepper flakes, plus more to taste (optional)

1 tablespoon dried oregano

1 tablespoon dried basil

2 teaspoons honey or granulated sugar

1 pound gluten-free or regular spaghetti (I love Garofalo or Jovial gluten-free pasta, often available at Barney's Market.)

½ cup stemmed and thinly sliced fresh basil

TIPS FOR SUCCESS

*You'll want quality fresh seafood for this recipe. In Harbor Country, the best spot to buy seafood is Flagship Specialty Foods and Fish Market, wonderfully curated by chef and owner Rachel Collins.*

*Wet versus Dry Packed Scallops: Scallops are often soaked in a phosphate solution that whitens them and makes them absorb more liquid, increasing their weight by as much as 30 percent. So you're paying $15 to $20 (or more) per pound for water. Also, that phosphate solution is a common ingredient in soaps and detergents, and not surprisingly, has a distinctly soap-like flavor. When you cook these scallops, all that extra liquid drains out and into the pan, so instead of searing them, if that's your goal, you end up steaming them in something closely resembling soapy water. To avoid that, look for scallops labeled "chemical-free" or "dry packed."*

*If using fresh calamari, clean it by removing the skin and separating the tentacles from the long body. Remove the innards, cuttlebone, and beak at the center of the tentacles, then the eyes, and finally slice the squid thinly.*

*Most Italians typically don't mix cheese and seafood, so avoid sprinkling with Parmesan to keep it real.*

**Make the Baking Pouch** Roll out a sheet of parchment paper or heavy-duty aluminum foil, about 2 feet long. Set aside.

**Prep** Preheat the oven to 375°F. In a large, covered pasta pot, bring 6 to 8 quarts of water, 1 tablespoon of the salt, and 1 tablespoon of the olive oil to a boil over high heat.

**Prepare the Seafood** While the water comes to a boil, pat the calamari, scallops, and shrimp dry with paper towels and set aside. Keep each seafood variety apart from the others, as you'll cook them separately.

**Make the Sauce** In a large sauté pan, heat the remaining ⅓ cup of olive oil over medium heat. Add the garlic and sauté about 2 minutes, or until just golden. Crush the plum tomatoes into the pan with your hands and add the cherry tomatoes, parsley, red pepper flakes (if using), oregano, basil, honey, and remaining 2 teaspoons of salt. Stir to combine. Continue to cook the sauce over medium heat for 10 minutes, stirring occasionally, while you cook the pasta.

*Recipe continues* ⟶

*Third Coast Seafood Pasta Baked in Parchment (Continued)*

**Cook the Pasta** Drop the pasta into the pot of boiling water, stir a few times to ensure the noodles separate, and return the water to a boil.

*Special Note: Cook pasta for two-thirds of the time called for on your pasta package; i.e., if it calls for 12 minutes, cook for 8 minutes. This will ensure it doesn't overcook in the oven.*

Drain the pasta, reserving 1½ cups of the pasta water. Set the pasta and reserved pasta water aside. Drizzle the cooked pasta liberally with olive oil to prevent it from sticking together. (If it does stick together, run some hot water over the pasta before placing it in the parchment paper.)

**Cook the Seafood** Increase the heat to medium-high and spread the calamari evenly over the tomato sauce in the sauté pan. Add ½ cup of the pasta water, stir to combine, and cook for about 2 minutes. Scatter the scallops evenly over the sauce. Add ½ cup of the pasta water, stir to combine, and cook for about 2 minutes. Add the shrimp to the pan, evenly spacing it over the sauce, and let cook for about 30 seconds per side. Now add the last ½ cup of the pasta water and stir to combine. Remove from the heat.

**Add the Pasta to the Sauce** Using a pasta fork or two large forks, add the pasta to the seafood sauce, working in batches. Gently toss the pasta with the sauce, ensuring the sauce coats the pasta evenly.

**Bake in the Parchment Pouch** Transfer the seafood pasta to the parchment paper or foil pouch, pulling the long edges of the paper or foil inward and folding them over the pasta to form a sealed pouch. Twist the short ends of the pouch to close. For extra "host with the most" points, you can also divide the seafood pasta evenly among smaller sheets of parchment paper to make individual pouches for your guests and serve the pouches on each plate. Place the filled pouch(es) on a baking sheet and bake for 6 minutes. The parchment paper might puff up slightly, which is normal.

**Let's Eat!** Remove the pouch(es) from the oven and slide them onto a large serving dish (or put one single serving pouch onto each plate) and place the dish in the center of the dining table, opening it dramatically to impress all your guests! *Special Note: Hot steam will rise once opened, so avoid having your face directly over the pouches.*

Sprinkle with the fresh basil and serve with extra red pepper flakes (if using) for all the heat seekers!

# Salmon Makes Miso Happy

IN HARBOR COUNTRY, local farmstands and most local grocery stories stock large jars of pickled vegetables. I never thought about the culinary possibilities of pickled vegetable juice until one summer weekend in New Buffalo. I had just picked up an envy-worthy fillet of salmon from Flagship Specialty Foods and Fish Market for a small dinner party I was hosting. Back home, I opened the fridge to see what ingredients called to me. There I spotted a jar of pickled beets with only the ruby-red juice remaining, and I saw sunset-colored fish in our immediate future. I whisked together the earthy, tangy beet juice, savory red miso paste, and sweet maple syrup, then marinated the salmon for about six hours. Each fillet developed a deep pink hue, and I baked them with fresh fennel bulbs from **Granor Farm** and garnished them with the feathery, lime-green fennel fronds. David wasn't totally sold on eating bright-fuchsia fish, but after one bite, he became a believer, and I think you will, too!

★ Granor Farm

3480 Warren Woods Rd. | Three Oaks, MI

Berrien County is known to be one of the most diverse growing regions in America for produce. Many farmstands can be found along the country roads, where farmers open pop-up shops for the growing season to sell what's been freshly harvested to anyone passing by. One of my favorite farmstands is located at the certified organic Granor Farm. One trip is enough to gain inspiration for an entire week of veggie-forward meals. Granor Farm also offers an incredible CSA program in the summer and fall. If you want to make a special trip to any farmstand in Harbor Country, call ahead to check their hours of operation or ask what produce is currently available.

# Beet-Red Sunset Salmon with Miso, Maple, and Roasted Fennel

**¶¶ 4** summer-loving servings    **45 min** active time    **8 hrs 45 min** start to finish

1 (2-pound) salmon fillet, center cut (Use a thicker salmon like king or Atlantic from a sustainable farm.)

8 tablespoons red or white miso paste, divided (I love Great Eastern Sun brand.)

⅓ cup maple syrup

3 cups pickled beet juice (Get this from 3 [15-ounce] cans or 1 large jar. If you can't find pickled beet juice, use plain and add 2 tablespoons red wine vinegar or rice vinegar to the juice.)

½ teaspoon ground cayenne pepper (optional for heat seekers)

1 shallot, or 3 cloves garlic, peeled and minced

2 tablespoons olive oil, plus more for coating baking pans

2 bulbs fresh fennel, stalks removed and sliced into ⅓-inch-thick pieces (Reserve and roughly chop the fennel fronds for garnish.)

Kosher or sea salt and freshly ground black pepper, to taste

TIPS FOR SUCCESS
*When cooked properly, salmon should flake apart with a fork and be moist and slightly translucent in the very center. Fish will continue to cook for another 5 minutes or so once removed from the oven, so to avoid overcooking, remove from the oven when the fish feels firm but still springs back to the touch.*

**Marinate 6 to 8 Hours**  If the salmon fillet is in one piece, place it skin side up on a cutting board. Using a sharp knife, cut it into 4 to 6 similar-size pieces to ensure even baking. Place the salmon skin side down in a glass baking dish. In a small bowl, whisk together 4 tablespoons of the miso paste and the maple syrup. Brush the fish liberally with the miso-maple paste to coat the top and sides of the salmon. In a medium bowl, whisk together the beet juice, the remaining 4 tablespoons of miso paste, the cayenne (if using), and the shallot. Pour the beet marinade around the salmon in the baking dish, leaving the thicker paste on top of the fish untouched. Cover with aluminum foil or plastic wrap and refrigerate for 6 to 8 hours maximum.

**Prep the Salmon to Bake**  Remove the salmon from the refrigerator 30 minutes before baking. Preheat the oven to 425°F and line a baking sheet with foil, then brush it with oil. Use a basting brush to sweep the excess miso paste from the top of the salmon and place the fish, skin side down, in the center of the prepared baking sheet, with the slices evenly spaced. Set aside.

**Prep the Fennel**  In a medium bowl, toss the sliced fennel with the olive oil and sprinkle with salt and pepper. Arrange the dressed fennel slices around the salmon along the edges of the baking sheet and scatter a few pieces of fennel over the top.

**Bake the Salmon**  Bake on the middle rack of the oven for 10 to 12 minutes, until the internal temperature of the salmon is 120°F to 125°F. Do not overcook or the salmon will be dry and chewy.

**Let's Eat!**  Once done, remove from the oven, plate with the roasted fennel, and garnish with the fennel fronds. You can also serve this dish with my Roasted Jalapeño Pecan Asparagus with Lemon Zest (page 74). Then sit back and bask in the vibrant glow of your sunset-inspired dinner!

# Roasting and Boasting

ONE OF OUR favorite Sunday night rituals at Camp Navama is curling up to watch any food-driven docuseries we haven't already devoured. We have *Chef's Table* to thank for helping us discover Chef Francis Mallmann, man of mystery and king of open-fire cooking. From our couch in New Buffalo, we were transported to his remote island in Patagonia, where he prepares five-star feasts his way, using the most primal methods and simple ingredients: air, wood, smoke, fire, meat, vegetables, bread, cheese, eggs, butter, salt, and of course wine.

"We're cooking dinner in our fire pit tomorrow night." David said, mesmerized by the wild flames dancing beneath whole chickens onscreen.

At sunset the next day, with far more confidence than we should have had, David built a roaring fire in our small fire pit and I got started cooking. I seasoned the fish and vegetables simply, with sea salt, citrus, fresh herbs, olive oil, and butter. We wrapped our feast foods in aluminum foil parcels, buried them under the hot ash, and waited. About 45 minutes later we plucked the blackened foil bundles from the smoldering fire, opening them tentatively.

Thankfully, there was no need to order emergency Chinese takeout. The squash was caramelized, the onions buttery, and the fish, on the flames for just 20 minutes, was tender and flaky. We relished every bite of the rustic open-air meal, sitting in our Adirondack chairs and looking for the first stars to appear. When you're ready for your own Chef Mallmann moment, watch the episode, light a fire, pour some wine, and cook with a generous splash of wild abandon.

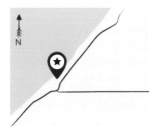

★ Skip's New Buffalo European Farmers Market

16710 Lakeshore Rd. | New Buffalo, MI

We picked up our onions, apples, and zucchini for this recipe from Skip's New Buffalo European Farmers Market. Each weekend from May to October, a wide variety of vendors, artisans, and farmers gather in front of the iconic Skip's Restaurant on Red Arrow Highway for this special farmers market, adored by locals and visitors alike.

# Seasonal Fire Pit Seafood Feast

🍴 **4–6** primal servings  ⏳ **2 hrs** start to finish

SPECIAL ITEMS NEEDED

Fire pit

Heavy-duty aluminum foil

Long cooking tongs

Dry hardwood

---

2–3 types of in-season vegetables of choice (see Freestyle box)

1 in-season fruit of choice (see Freestyle box)

Olive oil

Kosher salt and freshly ground black pepper, to taste

Spices and fresh herbs of choice (see Freestyle box)

3–4 pounds fish of choice, cut into ½-pound portions (see Freestyle box)

TIPS FOR SUCCESS

*The best cooking fire is mostly hot ash/coals with a few logs of burning wood. During roasting, continue to add wood as needed to keep a small fire going in the center of the fire pit.*

*Do not put foil packages directly on the flames or the foil can become brittle and split open. Wrap the food well to prevent ashes from getting inside the foil and ruining your feast!*

*Bury winter squash and root vegetables that take longer to cook deeper under the hot ash and closer to the fire. Roast fish in the "medium" heat areas, a bit farther from the fire's center, and fruit in the cooler areas on the outer edge of the ashes.*

*Keep a fresh bucket of water nearby for fire safety. Douse the fire with water once cooking is finished.*

**Prepare the Fire Pit** Build your fire about 35 to 45 minutes before you plan to begin roasting. The fire needs to burn down to create a hot bed of ash.

**Oil and Season the Vegetables and Fruit** Lay out sheets of heavy-duty aluminum foil, about 12 inches long, one for each type of vegetable or fruit you are roasting, and more if needed depending on quantity. Brush the vegetables and fruit with oil and sprinkle with salt, pepper, spices, and fresh herbs as desired. Make a foil package by bringing each long side together, then folding down to make a seam, before folding the ends in toward the center to seal the rectangular pouch. It's important to seal the pouch tightly so no ash touches the vegetables and fruit.

**Oil and Season the Fish** Lay out sheets of heavy-duty aluminum foil, about 12 inches long, one for each piece of fish you are roasting. Brush the fish with oil and sprinkle with salt, pepper, spices, and fresh herbs as desired. Make a foil package by bringing each long side together, then folding down to make a seam before folding the ends in toward the center to seal the rectangular pouch. It's important to seal the pouch tightly so no ash touches the fish.

**Roast the Produce and Fish** Roast the vegetables, which will take the longest, first, followed by the fish, then the fruit (see Roasting Times table in the Freestyle box on page 28). Place the foil packages in the ashes around the fire, not directly on the flames. If you can't fit all the vegetable, fish, and fruit packages into the fire pit at once, roast the vegetables first, then remove them. They can be kept warm in the oven at 250°F while the fish and fruit roast.

Use long tongs to turn the foil packages two to three times during the cooking process for even roasting. Always use tongs to remove the foil from the fire, as the packages are VERY HOT! Hot steam can rise from the packages when opened, so do not place your face directly over the packages.

**Let's Eat!** After the packages cool slightly, use a knife to make a slit in the pouch center and remove the vegetables and fruit from the foil. Place on serving trays so guests can help themselves. Place one foil package of fish on each super lucky guest's plate so they can have fun opening their own fire pit–roasted pouch. Have them use knives to open the pouches. Consider sprinkling the fish with seasoning salt to taste. Accept your "Most Adventurous Cook" award as your guests raise a glass to yet another memorable meal.

*Recipe continues* ⇒⇒⇒⟶

## Freestyle

Choose your vegetables, fruit, and fish in portions large enough to feed four to six people. For example, to feed four to six people, use 4 zucchini, 4 ears of corn (shucked and halved), 2 bundles of asparagus, and 4 peaches (pitted and halved).

Stone fruit, apples, and pears hold up well when roasted. Wash, prep, and cut the fruit and vegetables as needed.

**Berrien County Spring/Summer Produce**

Peaches, Asparagus, Beets, Broccoli, Carrots, Corn, Zucchini, Summer Squash

**Berrien County Fall Produce**

Apples, Grapes, Brussels Sprouts, Beets, Broccoli, Onions, Potatoes, Sugar Pumpkin, Winter Squash

**Fish**

Choose a hearty fish, such as salmon, white fish, halibut, sturgeon, black cod, or swordfish, but avoid fish that is too delicate, like sole. *A good seasoning formula per piece of fish is 1/4 teaspoon salt, 1/4 teaspoon pepper, and 1/2 teaspoon spices or 1 teaspoon minced garlic or onion.*

**Vegetable/Fruit Combinations**

Beets + Hazelnut Oil + Salt + Minced Candied Ginger

Zucchini + Olive Oil + Crushed Fennel Seeds + Salt + Red Pepper Flakes

Sugar Pumpkin + Ground Nutmeg + Ground Cloves + Salt + Pepper

Pears Stuffed with Raspberries + Olive Oil + Balsamic Glaze

**Fish Combinations**

Salmon + Olive Oil + Brown Sugar + Salt + Minced Garlic

White Fish + Walnut Oil + Dill + Lemon Pepper + Salt

Black Cod + Sesame Oil + Sesame Seeds + Orange Slices + Tamari

**Roasting Times**

Winter Squash/Pumpkin/Potatoes/Root Vegetables: 30 to 45 minutes roasted in foil under the ashes with the fire still burning

Green Vegetables/Corn/Zucchini: 20 to 30 minutes roasted in foil under the ashes with the fire still burning

Fish: 15 to 20 minutes roasted in foil under the ashes with the fire still burning, or until the internal temperature of the fish reaches 125°F to 135°F, depending on the fish

Fruit: 10 to 20 minutes roasted in foil under the ashes with the fire still burning

# Will Shepherd for Pie

I N MANY WAYS, my husband David has been my shepherd. When we met, I was feeling adrift in the world, lost about where to go next. At just 25 years old, however, he was confident, clear on his intentions, and committed to his goals. Together we learned to navigate life's trails, which eventually led us to this magical place called Harbor Country.

Most nights, right before we fall asleep, David will roll over and say, "I have a vision." He then proceeds to describe in great detail either a new idea or a classic craving he has for a dinner or dessert I should make the next night. At first I thought this was a phase, but several years in, these "dinner visions" remain our nightly form of pillow talk.

"Why haven't you ever made shepherd's pie?!" he half asked, half accused me late one night. "I saw a chef on TV making one, and it looked so good!" Thanks to his pesky allergies, we're always on the lookout for new gluten- and cow dairy–free recipes. He simply could not believe I'd never made this "David-friendly" dish.

Don't let the long recipe intimidate you. Make it once and you'll see it's both easy and addictive!

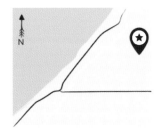

★ **Dinges' Fall Harvest**

15219 Mill Rd. | Three Oaks, MI

If you happen to have a craving for shepherd's pie during the autumn months, Dinges' Fall Harvest has some of the best butternut squash around.

# Checkerboard Shepherd's Pie with Bison

🍴 **8–10** hearty servings  🕐 **1 hr 30 min** active time  ⧖ **2 hrs 40 min** start to finish

SPECIAL ITEMS NEEDED

2 large cast iron skillets, or
1 (9 × 12-inch) oven-safe baking
dish with minimum 3-inch sides

Food processor or high-
powered blender

Piping bags with large star tips,
if you want to pipe potatoes and
squash

BUTTERNUT SQUASH

2 tablespoons olive oil or
neutral oil, like grapeseed oil,
plus more for brushing pan

1 large or 2 small butternut squash,
seeded, peeled, and cubed into
1-inch pieces (about 4 cups)

2 tablespoons dairy-free
milk or milk of choice

2 tablespoons salted butter

1 egg yolk

1 teaspoon kosher salt

½ teaspoon freshly ground black
pepper, plus more to taste

½ teaspoon ground nutmeg (optional)

POTATOES

3 medium russet potatoes, peeled,
halved lengthwise, and cubed into
1-inch pieces (about 1½ pounds)

2½ teaspoons kosher salt, divided

⅓ cup dairy-free milk or milk
of choice

3 tablespoons salted butter

1 teaspoon freshly ground black
pepper, plus more to taste

1 teaspoon honey or granulated
sugar

½ teaspoon ground nutmeg
(optional)

⅛ teaspoon ground cayenne pepper

1 egg yolk

TIPS FOR SUCCESS

*Use mise en place. This recipe looks long, but it's actually pretty simple, and mise en place will help the process go more quickly and smoothly. This is helpful for any recipe, but especially for those with more ingredients and steps. It also requires you to read the whole recipe before beginning, which is important to ensure delicious success!*

**Prepare the Butternut Squash**  Preheat the oven to 400°F. Line a baking sheet with parchment paper or aluminum foil and brush with oil. Arrange the butternut squash in an even layer on the baking sheet, drizzle with 2 tablespoon of the oil, and roast for 20 to 30 minutes until easily pierced with fork. Remove from the oven and let cool 5 minutes. (Keep the oven at 400°F to cook the pie later.)

Place the squash in the bowl of a standing mixer with the paddle attachment. Beat on medium speed until just mashed, 30 seconds to 1 minute. Add the milk, butter, egg yolk, salt, pepper, and nutmeg (if using) and mix on medium speed until blended, 1 to 2 minutes. Do not overmix or the butternut squash will be starchy. Transfer the squash to another bowl and set aside. (Alternatively, place the squash in a medium bowl and mash using a hand mixer or potato masher.)

**Boil the Potatoes**  While squash roasts, place the potatoes in a medium pot and cover with cold water. Add 1 teaspoon of the salt and stir. Cover and bring to a boil over high heat. Once the potatoes are boiling, uncover and reduce the heat to maintain a simmer. Cook until just tender and easily crushed with fork, 25 to 30 minutes.

**Heat the Butter and Milk**  Drain the potatoes in a colander. While the potatoes drain, place the remaining 1½ teaspoons salt, the milk, the butter, the pepper, the honey, the nutmeg (if using), and the cayenne into a small pot. Over medium heat, whisk continually until the butter is melted and the ingredients are combined. Remove from the heat and set aside.

**Mash the Potatoes**  Place the drained potatoes in the bowl of a standing mixer. Using the paddle attachment, beat the potatoes on medium speed for about 30 seconds, then add the hot milk mixture and continue to beat on medium speed until smooth (about 1 minute), scraping the bowl with a spatula as needed. Do not overbeat. Mix in the egg yolk until combined, 30 seconds to 1 minute. There will be small lumps in the potatoes, and that's okay! No potato is perfect. Set aside. (Alternatively, return the potatoes to the pot once drained, pour in the hot milk mixture, and mash using a hand mixer or potato masher.)

3 tablespoons olive
oil or avocado oil

1½ medium red onions,
peeled and chopped

4 large carrots, peeled and diced

4 cloves garlic, minced

2 teaspoons kosher salt

2 pounds ground bison (Use
ground beef, if preferred.)

3 tablespoons tandoori spice
powder (In a pinch, use
any curry spice blend.)

2 teaspoons fennel seeds,
crushed (In a pinch, use
1 teaspoon ground fennel.)

1 teaspoon ground ginger

½ teaspoon red pepper flakes
(optional for heat seekers)

½ teaspoon freshly
ground black pepper

3 tablespoons cornstarch, rice
flour, or regular all-purpose flour

1 cup beef, chicken, or
vegetable broth

¼ cup tomato paste

¼ cup ketchup

2 tablespoons
Worcestershire sauce

1½ cups fresh or frozen
corn kernels

2 cups fresh or frozen green peas

2 cups fresh or frozen cut okra
(If fresh, cut into ½-inch rounds.)

FOR SERVING

¾ cup thinly sliced green
onions, for garnish (optional)

**Make the Pie Filling**  Add the oil to a large pot over medium-high heat. Once the oil shimmers, add the onions and carrots, then cover and cook 5 to 7 minutes, stirring occasionally. Add the garlic and salt, stir to combine, and cook another 3 minutes. Add the bison and use a spatula to crumble. Sprinkle the tandoori, fennel, ginger, red pepper flakes, and black pepper into the pot, then stir to coat the meat and vegetables with the spices. Reduce the heat to medium and cook until the meat is browned, 5 to 6 minutes. Sprinkle the meat with the cornstarch and stir to coat, cooking for another 2 minutes. Add the broth, tomato paste, ketchup, and Worcestershire sauce and stir to combine. Bring to a boil, reduce the heat to low, cover, and simmer for 10 to 12 minutes, until the sauce thickens slightly. Add the corn, peas, and okra to the bison mixture and use a spatula or wooden spoon to fold in gently. Remove from the heat.

**Put That Pie Together!**  Fill an oven-safe baking dish with the meat filling in one even layer, leaving at least 1 inch of room from the brim of the dish for the potatoes and squash. Place spoonfuls of potato around the edge of the baking dish or skillet to create a seal that will prevent the meat mixture from bubbling up. Make a "ring" of potato, then a "ring" of squash, alternating and moving toward the center, until the meat is completely covered. Use a small spatula or the back of a spoon to create a "scalloped" look on the potatoes and squash if you're feeling fancy! For a more rustic look, just smooth out the potato and squash rings a bit, ensuring no meat shows through. Alternatively, follow the steps in the Freestyle box to pipe the squash and potatoes over the meat filling.

**Bake the Pie**  Place the pie on the center oven rack and bake for 25 to 30 minutes, or just until the potato and squash topping begins to brown. Remove from the oven and pat yourself on the back for completing a long but worth-it recipe.

**Let's Eat!**  Let cool for about 15 minutes before serving. Sprinkle the top with the green onions (if using) and serve immediately!

## Freestyle

### Pipe the Potatoes and Squash

If you want to serve a whimsical shepherd's pie that will make your guests ooh and ahh, take the extra time to pipe your potatoes and squash! For the butternut squash, once roasted, add the squash, milk, butter, salt, egg yolk, black pepper, and nutmeg (if using) to a high-powered blender or food processor and blend until just smooth. For the potatoes, rice them before placing in a standing mixer with the milk mixture and beat on medium for only 1 minute, or until just combined. Fit two medium or large pastry bags with large star-style pastry tips, at least 1 inch in diameter. Fill one bag two-thirds full of potatoes and one two-thirds full of squash. Starting on the outside of the baking dish, pipe "star shapes" (see photo on page 31 for an example) with the potatoes along the edges to create a seal and prevent the meat from bubbling up. Next, pipe a ring of squash "stars" inside the potatoes and alternate the potatoes and squash, moving toward the center, until the meat is completely covered.

*Recipe continues*  ⇒⇒⇒⟶

*Checkerboard Shepherd's Pie with Bison (continued)*

## Freestyle

Short on time? Consider making this potatoes-only option using the ingredients below. Just follow the same directions in this recipe, but omit the step of preparing the squash.

**Potatoes-Only Option**

5 medium-large russet potatoes, peeled (about 2½ pounds)

4 teaspoons kosher salt, divided

½ cup dairy-free milk or milk of choice

5 tablespoons salted butter

1 egg yolk

1½ teaspoons freshly ground black pepper

1 teaspoon honey or granulated sugar

1 teaspoon nutmeg (optional)

¼ teaspoon ground cayenne pepper

# Low and Slow We Go

WHILE LIVING IN Los Angeles, we were treated to sumptuous shabbat dinners at David's parents' house every Friday night, and brisket was among the many delicious meals they cooked for us.

My version of brisket, inspired by the Rosh Hashanah and Passover celebrations my husband had growing up, is a hybrid of two methods: BBQ and low and slow oven roasting. In the spirit of autumn—and because I had four bags of local apples haunting my tiny kitchen—I replaced the typical potatoes with sliced apples spiced with cinnamon, nutmeg, and cloves, as well as some whiskey. Barbecuing the brisket creates a thick seared crust before roasting, adding a terrific texture to the final dish and helping to seal in the critical juiciness during the long roasting fiesta.

The thing to know about brisket is that, when it's prepared well, it's melt-in-your-mouth amazing. But most brisket requires patience, and if you rush the cooking process, you'll get an inedible hunk of protein that's drier than a parched piggy in the Sahara Desert. Prepare this recipe on a day when you make time to start early, take it slow, and enjoy the process.

### ★ Kaminski Farms

16682 S. Schwark Rd | Three Oaks, MI

One of the amazing things about living near so many farms is the access to locally grown and raised food, including meat. Kaminski Farms, located in Three Oaks, is my go-to place to buy beef, poultry, and, on occasion, lamb. They also have terrific, hard-to-find soup bones for making your own stock in the colder winter months. Owned by husband and wife David and Linda Kaminski, the store is generally open from 10 a.m. to 3 p.m., but call ahead, as this is a working farm and sometimes the storefront opens late or closes early.

# Whiskey Apple Brisket with Spiced Carrots and Onions

**8–10** rich and rustic servings    **1 hr** active time    **9 hrs 20 min** start to finish, plus 8 hrs to dry brine (optional)

SPECIAL ITEMS NEEDED

Large roasting pan

---

Brisket

1 (6-pound) brisket, center cut preferred (Buy locally at Kaminski Farms.)

¼ cup paprika

3 tablespoons light or dark brown sugar

2 tablespoons plus 2 teaspoons kosher salt, divided

2 tablespoons chili powder

1 tablespoon plus 2 teaspoons freshly ground black pepper, divided

1 tablespoon ground cumin

1 tablespoon onion powder

3 medium red onions, peeled and sliced into ½-inch-thick rings

8 large carrots, peeled and cut into 1-inch rounds

3 medium apples, cored and sliced into ½-inch-thick rings (Use baking apples such as Pink Lady, Jonagold, Honeycrisp, or Winesap.)

2 tablespoons stemmed and minced thyme or sage

1 tablespoon ground cinnamon

2 teaspoons ground nutmeg

1 teaspoon ground cloves

½ cup whiskey

WHISKEY PAN SAUCE

2 tablespoons whiskey

1 tablespoon marmalade or honey

**Prep and Season the Brisket** If you're a flavor fanatic, dry brine the brisket the night before roasting. Using a sharp chef's knife, trim the fat layer evenly to be about ⅓ inch to ½ inch thick, or have the butcher do this for you.

For the dry rub, in a small bowl, mix together the paprika, the brown sugar, 2 tablespoons of the salt, the chili powder, 1 tablespoon of the pepper, the cumin, and the onion powder. Season the brisket liberally with the spice mixture on all sides. If seasoning in advance, wrap the meat tightly in plastic wrap and refrigerate for at least 6 to 8 hours. Remove the brisket from the refrigerator 1 hour before grilling, remove the plastic wrap, and let it come to room temperature. *Special Note: If tight on time, season the brisket just before cooking and let it rest, unwrapped, for about 1 hour, to come to room temperature.*

**Preheat the Oven** Arrange the oven rack in the center position of the oven. About 30 minutes before searing the brisket, preheat the grill to about 450°F and preheat the oven to 225°F.

**Arrange the Apples and Vegetables** While the brisket comes to room temperature, arrange the onions, carrots, and apples in an even layer in the bottom of a large roasting pan. Sprinkle with the thyme, cinnamon, nutmeg, the remaining 2 teaspoons of salt, the remaining 2 teaspoons of pepper, and the cloves. Toss to distribute the seasoning. Pour the whiskey into the pan. Set aside.

**Cut and Sear the Brisket** Brush the grill with oil. Once the grill reaches 450°F, sear the brisket, fat side down first, for about 5 to 6 minutes per side, until a browned crust forms. Use tongs to flip the brisket and press the edges down to ensure even searing. Once browned, remove the brisket from the grill and transfer it to a cutting board. Cut the brisket in half crosswise before searing.

**Slow Cook the Brisket in the Oven** Place the seared brisket, *fat side up*, on top of the vegetables in the roasting pan and cover tightly with aluminum foil. In the oven, slow roast the brisket for 6 to 8 hours, until the internal temperature reaches about 175°F. Resist the urge to check it before the 6-hour mark. Remove the brisket from the oven when it jiggles slightly with a gentle shake of the roasting pan. Once removed from the oven, rest for 30 minutes. Transfer the brisket to a cutting board and reserve the braising liquid for the whiskey pan sauce. Reserve the apples and vegetables for serving. Using a sharp carving knife, slice pieces about ⅓ inch thick *against the grain of the brisket*.

**Make the Whiskey Pan Sauce** In a small saucepan over medium-high heat, whisk together 1½ cups of the braising liquid, the whiskey, and the marmalade. Bring to a simmer, whisking often. Reduce the heat to low and simmer for 5 minutes. If you have a lot of braising liquid, feel free to double this recipe.

**Let's Eat!** Arrange the brisket slices on a serving platter. Place the apples, onions, and carrots around the brisket so your guests can help themselves to both the star of the show and the supporting cast members. Ladle some of the leftover braising liquid over the brisket and serve the whiskey pan sauce on the side. Savor the night.

TIPS FOR SUCCESS

*Ask your butcher for the
middle cut of a whole brisket.*

*No grill? No worries! Instead of
using a grill, heat a large cast
iron or stainless steel skillet on
the stovetop over high heat.
Add about 1 tablespoon olive
oil, reduce the heat to medium-
high, and sear each side of the
brisket for 4 to 6 minutes.*

# Power to the Cauliflower

THEY SAY HARBOR COUNTRY is a place where you can express yourself. It's also a place where you can find buffalo wings at more restaurants than not. Some of our favorite spots for wings are the delicious Red Arrow Roadhouse, The Stray Dog Bar & Grill, and Greenbush Brewing Co. While always crispy and delicious, these wings are typically fried. Ever on a quest to make creative cuisine that's healthy-ish and delish, I decided to jump on the "cauliflower buffalo wing" trend train because I wasn't willing to get into the frying game at home.

One night, our friend Susan served a whole roasted head of cauliflower at one of her RDI (or Red Door Inn, the name of her lovely lake house) dinner parties. I decided it might be magical to create one giant buffalo-battered cauliflower head (with cauliflower from **Barney's Market**), blanketed in BBQ sauce with bacon, Cheddar, and potato chip crumbles. (Hey, at least it's not fried!)

Serve the head whole, allowing your guests to savor the drama, then slice everyone a wedge and toast to this new way to enjoy buffalo bliss.

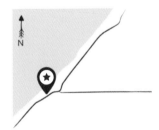

★ Barney's Market

10 N. Thompson St. | New Buffalo, MI

I'm pretty sure I cleared Barney's Market of cauliflower several days in a row while I developed this delicious vision into an actual recipe—but oh, my friends, it was worth it! This local grocery store has an excellent variety of products, whether you're making a simple roast chicken dinner or need to pick up a unique spice for a more exotic recipe.

# Whole Roasted Buffalo Cauliflower with Bacon Potato Chip Crumble

🍴 **4–8** craveable servings   🕐 **30 min** active time   ⏳ **1 hr 35 min** start to finish

## BACON AND CAULIFLOWER

2 tablespoons olive oil, plus more for brushing baking sheets

6–8 pieces thick-cut bacon, uncured if available

1 medium head cauliflower

1 teaspoon kosher salt, plus more to taste

## BATTER

1 cup gluten-free all-purpose flour *without* xanthan gum or regular all-purpose flour (I use King Arthur All-Purpose Gluten-Free Flour or Bob's Red Mill Gluten-Free All-Purpose Baking Flour.)

1 teaspoon onion powder or garlic powder

½ teaspoon kosher salt

¼ teaspoon baking powder

⅛ teaspoon ground cayenne pepper

½ teaspoon ground white pepper

¼ cup water

2 tablespoons olive oil

2 tablespoons favorite wing sauce

½ cup almond milk or milk of choice, plus more as needed to create desired consistency for batter

## TOPPING

½ cup favorite BBQ sauce

2 tablespoons buffalo wing sauce

1 cup kettle-style BBQ potato chips

½ cup shredded Cheddar goat cheese or Cheddar of choice

½ cup finely chopped green onions

½ teaspoon freshly ground black pepper

**Prep**  Place the oven rack in the center position of the oven. Preheat the oven to 400°F. Line two baking sheets with aluminum foil or parchment paper. Brush one sheet liberally with olive oil. Line a large plate with two layers of paper towels. Set aside.

**Cook the Bacon**  Place the bacon strips in a single layer on the lined baking sheet *without oil* and bake until crisp, 20 to 25 minutes, depending on the thickness of the bacon. Transfer the bacon in a single layer to the prepared plate to cool.

**Prep and Roast the Cauliflower**  Raise the oven heat to 450°F. Using a large chef's knife, remove any leaves from the cauliflower head. Turn the head upside down and slice off the stem, slicing flush with the bottom of the cauliflower so it sits flat when right side up. Place on the oiled baking sheet and drizzle 1 tablespoon of the olive oil on the head, then turn over and drizzle the remaining 1 tablespoon of olive oil on the bottom. Sprinkle inside and out with the salt. Place the cauliflower head right side up in the center of the baking sheet and roast in the oven for 30 minutes.

**Prepare the Batter**  While the cauliflower roasts, in a medium bowl, whisk together the flour, onion powder, salt, baking powder, cayenne, and white pepper. In a smaller bowl, whisk together the water, olive oil, and wing sauce. Add the milk to the wing sauce mixture and whisk to fully combine. Pour three-quarters of the liquid mixture into the bowl with the flour mixture and whisk until smooth, adding the remaining liquid as necessary to achieve a medium-thick consistency.

**Batter the Cauliflower**  Use two forks to turn the cauliflower head upside down and dip it in the batter, covering only the dome of the cauliflower head, not the bottom or inside. Press the head into the batter using the forks. (It's hot!) Return the cauliflower to the baking sheet, stem side down, and bake for another 15 minutes, or until the batter is hardened and golden.

**Prepare the Topping**  In a small bowl, combine the BBQ sauce and buffalo wing sauce, then set aside. Finely chop the cooked bacon, then set aside. Place the potato chips in a bag. Use a rolling pin or can to crush finely. In a medium bowl, toss together the bacon pieces, potato chips, shredded cheese, green onions, and pepper until all the ingredients are finely crushed.

**Brush with the Sauce and Broil**  Remove the cauliflower from the oven and use the basting brush to generously coat the entire battered area with about half of the buffalo and BBQ sauce mixture. Return to the oven for 5 minutes, or until the sauce is sticky. Remove the cauliflower from the oven. Set the oven to broil. Use your hands to press the potato chip mixture all over the cauliflower head. Return the cauliflower to the oven and broil for 3 to 4 minutes, watching carefully to ensure it doesn't burn. Remove from the oven for the final time and use two forks to move to a serving platter.

**Let's Eat!**  Cut this beautiful wonder into 4 wedges if this is the entrée, or 6 to 8 wedges if this is a side dish. Serve with a side of the BBQ buffalo wing sauce.

# Fall for All and All for Squash

DURING THE FALL it's difficult to resist preparing squash in some form most nights of the week, especially when you live just nine miles from **Dinges' Fall Harvest**. All summer long, we ride our bikes by the Dinges family's magical wonderland in Three Oaks, Michigan, waiting for pumpkin season to begin!

After about a month into our first fall in Harbor Country, however, David was suffering from squash fatigue, so I put on my apron and got to work. My kitchen was also well stocked with u-pick autumn apples, and I started using them in savory dishes because it turns out apple pie burnout does exist.

Roasted acorn squash is a dinner party host's best friend because it requires minimal effort but always manages to look beautifully dramatic on the plate. Stuff each little squash bowl with freshly picked apples caramelized in rich bacon goodness. Top them with shreds of your favorite cheese as you sink into the coziness of autumn at the lake.

This dish makes a hearty vegetable-forward dinner entrée, or you can cut the squash into quarters once roasted and serve as a side dish. The savory, sweet flavors also make this recipe a favorite with the brunch bunch. Spicy Bloody, anyone?

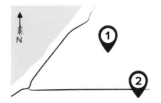

**1 Dinges' Fall Harvest**
15219 Mill Rd. | Three Oaks, MI

**2 Springhope Farm**
18720 Cleveland Ave. | Galien, MI

Dinges' Fall Harvest has piles of pumpkins, farm animals, and u-pick grapes along with an amazing variety of squash. For u-pick apples I head to the lovely Springhope Farm.

# Roasted Acorn Squash Bowls with Apple Bacon Pistachio Stuffing

🍴 **6** satisfying servings　🕐 **45 min** active time　⧗ **1 hr 45 min** start to finish

## BACON

8 ounces thick-cut bacon, uncured if available (Use turkey or vegan bacon, if preferred.)

## SQUASH

3 acorn squash of similar size

Olive oil

Kosher or sea salt and freshly ground black pepper, to taste

## STUFFING

4 tablespoons salted butter

3 large apples, peeled, cored, and diced into ½-inch cubes (Use tart baking apples such as Honeycrisp, Jonagold, or Granny Smith.)

½ cup diced shallots

½ cup diced red onion

¼ cup stemmed and finely chopped Italian parsley, plus more for garnish

1 tablespoon apple cider vinegar (In a pinch, use rice vinegar.)

2 teaspoons light or dark brown sugar (In a pinch, use granulated sugar.)

½ teaspoon ground cinnamon

½ teaspoon ground nutmeg or ground ginger

½ teaspoon kosher salt

Freshly ground black pepper, to taste

¾ cup chopped pistachios or nut of choice

## FOR SERVING

1½ cups shredded mozzarella of choice (I use goat milk mozzarella or Miyoko's Vegan Mozz.)

**TIPS FOR SUCCESS**

*Cut the apples, onion, and bacon into similar-size pieces to ensure your stuffing is top-notch in texture and flavor.*

**Prep**　Line two baking sheets with parchment paper or aluminum foil and set aside. Line a large plate with two layers of paper towels. Preheat the oven to 400°F.

**Cook the Bacon**　Place the bacon strips in a single layer on one of the prepared baking sheets and bake until crisp, 20 to 25 minutes, depending on the thickness of the bacon. Transfer the bacon in a single layer to the prepared plate to cool. Coarsely chop the cooked bacon into small pieces and set aside.

**Prep the Squash**　Raise the oven temperature to 425°F (on the roast setting, if you have one). Use a sharp chef's knife to slice each squash in half vertically, from stem to tip. Use a large spoon to remove the seeds and scoop out enough squash to make space for about ¾ cup stuffing.

Brush each squash half with olive oil, then sprinkle lightly with salt and pepper. Set the squash halves, bowl side down, on the second baking sheet. Roast for 30 minutes. While the squash bakes, make the stuffing.

**Make the Stuffing**　Melt the butter in a large sauté pan over medium-high heat. Add the apples, shallots, red onion, parsley, vinegar, sugar, cinnamon, nutmeg, salt, and pepper. Sauté over medium heat until the onion is translucent and the apples slightly soften, 8 to 10 minutes. Remove from the heat and fold in the chopped bacon and pistachios.

**Stuff the Squash and Finish Roasting**　Remove the squash from the oven, turn over, and divide the apple stuffing evenly among the squash halves. Return to the oven and roast for another 20 minutes, or until a knife tip easily pierces the squash flesh. Remove from the oven and sprinkle each squash with about ¼ cup of the mozzarella.

Turn the oven to broil on high. Return the squash to the oven and broil for about 3 minutes, or until the cheese has just melted, paying *close attention* to ensure it doesn't burn. Broiling can be amazing *or* disastrous, as my mom and I both know from experience—whoops!

**Let's Eat!**　Plate the squash and garnish with parsley to add a refreshing flavor and pop of green color.

# Easy and Light for Day or Night

ESPITE PRACTICALLY BECOMING a pop-up B&B, Camp Navama still delivered many moments of pure relaxation during our first Harbor Country summer. At the lake, there's a calm, casual energy that infuses most days, giving you permission to sleep in, nap often, and tuck in to a simple, locally grown kale salad or even pancakes for dinner.

This collection of recipes, ranging from cast iron skillet pancakes to my super simple, hyper-healthy pesto zucchini noodle salad, can be enjoyed for brunch, lunch, snack time, or dinner and require minimal effort to prepare. Visit this chapter often as you learn to stress less, live more, and treat yourself to delicious, homemade meals in Harbor Country and beyond.

P.S. If you think you don't like brussels sprouts, try my recipe on page 78. It's been known to completely change people's opinions about these miniature cabbages.

# Berry Proud of My Pancakes

I'VE NEVER LIKED flipping pancakes for a crowd. Without a large griddle, serving a bunch of people fluffy, piping hot, crispy-edge pancakes just isn't my idea of a relaxing Sunday morning. So as we prepared to host another round of guests at Camp Navama, I decided there had to be a better way to serve pancakes on Sunday morning while preserving my weekend zen.

Rummaging through my kitchen, waiting for inspiration to strike, I spotted the solution to my conundrum: the iconic cast iron skillet. I could bake one large pancake to serve family style! By putting the skillet in the oven to preheat before adding the butter and batter, you preserve both the crispy edges and fluffy texture, so critical to a really good pancake.

Our level of indulgence also changes from week to weekend and meal to meal. Sometimes we will 100 percent relish a plate of classic pancakes made with all the carbohydrates, like at Luisa's Café in Harbert! Other days, we steer our taste buds toward lighter foods, like these paleo-friendly pancakes, which are packed with protein to keep your paddle and play game strong all day long. True, the drizzle of white chocolate isn't paleo, but it is delicious. And now that David and I officially have "his and hers" pancakes, our marriage feels complete.

★ Garwood Orchards

5911 W. 50 S | La Porte, IN

During my first u-pick adventure at Garwood Orchards, one of my favorite farms to pick local produce, I shifted my berry loyalty from blueberries to the perfectly sweet-tart red raspberry. After all, one of my mottos is "Enjoy all foods and flavors, but tastes change from day to day—and that's perfectly okay."

# His Chocolate Blueberry Pancakes with Blueberry Bourbon Syrup

**¶1 4–6** growing boy servings　⏱ **25 min** active time　⧗ **40 min** start to finish

SPECIAL ITEMS NEEDED

10-inch cast iron skillet or oven-safe stainless steel skillet

BLUEBERRY BOURBON SYRUP

½ cup fresh blueberries

3 tablespoons maple syrup

2 tablespoons bourbon (I use Journeyman Featherbone Bourbon Whiskey.)

⅛ teaspoon kosher or sea salt

PANCAKE BATTER

1 tablespoon salted butter, plus more to butter skillet

¼ cup plus 2 tablespoons firmly packed almond flour

2 tablespoons coconut flour

¼ teaspoon baking powder

¼ teaspoon kosher salt

1 egg, at room temperature

3 egg whites, at room temperature

⅓ cup almond milk or milk of choice

2 tablespoons honey

½ teaspoon pure vanilla extract (optional)

⅓ cup fresh blueberries

¼ cup semisweet chocolate chips, divided

TIPS FOR SUCCESS

*These recipes make 1 large pancake each, and the recipes cannot be doubled. To make more than 1 pancake, just make and bake the batter twice.*

*Don't overmix, or your batter or pancake can get tough.*

**Prep**  Place the cast iron skillet in the oven on the middle rack and preheat to 375°F.

**Make the Blueberry Bourbon Syrup**  In a small saucepan, stir together the blueberries, maple syrup, bourbon, and salt. Bring to a boil over medium heat, then cover, reduce the heat to low, and simmer for about 10 minutes, or until the blueberries cook down and the syrup thickens. Remove from the heat and set aside.

**Make the Batter**  In a small ramekin, heat the butter for about 20 seconds in the microwave until it melts. Set aside to cool slightly. In a medium mixing bowl whisk together the almond flour, coconut flour, baking powder, and salt. Set aside.

In a small mixing bowl, use a fork to lightly beat the egg and egg whites. Stir in the melted butter, almond milk, honey, and vanilla extract (if using) until just combined. Add to the flour mixture and whisk until the batter is just combined and the larger lumps are gone. *Resist overmixing the batter to avoid a tough pancake!*

**Bake the Pancake**  Working quickly and using a heavy-duty oven mitt, remove the skillet from the oven. Please be very careful! This cast iron skillet is SUPER HOT. Leave the mitt over the handle to prevent grabbing it by accident. Lightly brush the skillet with about ½ teaspoon of butter to coat the bottom and sides evenly. Pour the batter into the skillet and gently shake it, or use a spatula to spread the batter into an even layer if necessary.

Scatter the blueberries and 2 tablespoons of the chocolate chips evenly over the batter. Return to the oven and bake for 12 to 15 minutes, until the pancake is springy to the touch and a toothpick inserted into the center comes out clean. Let cool 5 minutes, then loosen the edges with a rubber spatula.

**Add Some Pizzazz!**  In a small microwave-safe ramekin or bowl, heat the remaining 2 tablespoons of chocolate chips for 30 seconds, then stir and continue to microwave in 30-second increments until the chocolate is melted, smooth, and easily drizzles off a fork. This should take about 1 minute.

**Let's Eat!**  Drizzle or drench your pancakes with the blueberry syrup and melted chocolate—your call! Decide if you want to serve your family-style pancakes in the skillets (so fun!) or on a large plate (meh). Cut slices for all and smile as you indulge in what looks like dessert, but is actually nutritious, healthy-ish, and delicious!

Leftovers can be covered and refrigerated for 1 to 2 days. Reheat in the microwave for about 30 seconds.

# Her Raspberry White Chocolate Pancakes with Raspberry Sauce

🍴 **4–6** buttery, sweet, and tart servings ⏱ **25 min** active time ⧗ **40 min** start to finish

SPECIAL ITEMS NEEDED

10-inch cast iron skillet or oven-safe stainless steel skillet

RASPBERRY SAUCE

½ cup fresh raspberries

2–3 tablespoons honey
or granulated sugar

½ teaspoon pure vanilla extract

⅛ teaspoon kosher or sea salt

Zest of ½ lemon

PANCAKE BATTER

1 tablespoon salted butter,
plus more to butter skillet

¼ cup plus 2 tablespoons
firmly packed almond flour

2 tablespoons coconut flour

¼ teaspoon baking powder

¼ teaspoon kosher salt

¼ teaspoon ground nutmeg
(optional but awesome)

1 egg, at room temperature

3 egg whites, at room temperature

⅓ cup almond milk or
milk of choice

2 tablespoons honey,
agave, or maple syrup

¼ teaspoon almond extract
(optional but awesome)

3 tablespoons white
chocolate chips

About ⅓ cup fresh
raspberries, for garnish

Confectioners' sugar, for garnish
(optional but beautiful!)

**Prep** Place the cast iron skillet in the oven on the middle rack and preheat to 375°F.

**Make the Raspberry Sauce** In a small saucepan, stir together the raspberries, honey, vanilla, salt, and lemon zest, mashing the raspberries a bit with a spoon. Bring to a strong simmer over medium-high heat. Reduce the heat to medium-low and continue cooking for 10 to 15 minutes, until the raspberries break down and the sauce reduces. Remove from the heat and set aside.

**Make the Batter** In a small ramekin, heat the butter for about 20 seconds in the microwave until it melts. Set aside to cool slightly. In a medium mixing bowl, whisk together the almond flour, coconut flour, baking powder, salt, and nutmeg (if using). Set aside.

In a small mixing bowl, use a fork to lightly beat the egg and egg whites. Stir in the melted butter, almond milk, honey, and almond extract (if using) until combined. Add to the flour mixture and whisk until the batter is just combined and the larger lumps are gone. *Resist overmixing the batter to avoid a tough pancake!*

**Bake the Pancake** Working quickly and using a heavy-duty oven mitt, remove the skillet from the oven. Please be very careful! This cast iron skillet is SUPER HOT. Leave the mitt over the handle to prevent grabbing it by accident. Lightly brush the skillet with about ½ teaspoon of butter to coat the bottom and sides evenly. Pour the batter into the skillet and gently shake it, or use a spatula to spread the batter into an even layer if necessary.

Drizzle 2 tablespoons of the raspberry sauce over the batter and lightly swirl with a knife, if desired. Return to the oven and bake for 12 to 15 minutes, until the pancake is springy to the touch and a toothpick inserted into the center comes out clean. Let cool 5 minutes, then loosen the edges with a rubber spatula.

**Add Some Pizzazz!** In a small microwave-safe ramekin or bowl, heat the white chocolate chips for 30 seconds, then stir and continue to microwave in 20-second increments until the chocolate is melted, smooth, and easily drizzles off a fork. This should take about 1 minute.

**Let's Eat!** Dip a fork in the white chocolate and drizzle over the pancake in thin lines, then top with fresh raspberries and a light dusting of confectioners' sugar. Serve family-style pancakes in the skillets (so fun!) or on a large plate (meh). Cut slices for all and smile as you indulge in what looks like dessert, but is actually nutritious, healthy-ish, and delicious!

Leftovers can be covered and refrigerated for 1 to 2 days. Reheat in the microwave for about 30 seconds.

# Morning Glory

FOR ME, DISCOVERING new u-pick opportunities feels like finding huge treasure chests of golden cupcakes frosted with platinum—basically, the best thing on earth. So, you can imagine my super grin when I learned Harbor Country is located in one of America's fruit belts and that u-pick farms are as abundant here as steakhouses are in Chicago.

When we first started visiting the region, **Garwood Orchards**, located in Indiana, was our first u-pick stop. With my parents and friends visiting from California in tow, we climbed aboard a tractor wagon and were dropped off in a land of berry bliss! Within an hour our baskets were brimming and our bellies were full of juicy red raspberries, plump blackberries, and sweet blueberries.

Once "u-pick," you need to find a way to use all the fruit that you enthusiastically adopted while frolicking in the fields. I often suffer from the "no pumpkin left behind" mentality—but that's a story for another recipe. I decided to use some of my berries to make overnight oats. As nature's gumdrops, berries infuse the earthy oats with a sweet, bright flavor and vibrant color, turning your healthy but beige breakfast into one bowl of beautiful!

★ Garwood Orchards

5911 W. 50 S | La Porte, IN

Garwood Orchards has been run by the Garwood family for over 180 years, and their commitment to growing great fruits and vegetables can be tasted in every bite. From berries, cherries, and cucumbers in the summer to pumpkins and apples come fall, Garwood Orchards offers a wonderful variety of u-pick produce.

# U-Pick Berry Chai Overnight Oats

🍴 **4** nourishing servings    🕐 **30 min** active time    ⧗ **6 hrs** start to finish

SPECIAL ITEMS NEEDED

4 (16-ounce) mason jars

BERRY SAUCE

1¼ cups fresh berries, such as raspberries, blueberries, or blackberries

3 tablespoons honey or maple syrup

½ teaspoon kosher or sea salt

Zest of 1 orange or lemon

CHAI SPICE BLEND

1½ teaspoons ground cinnamon

1 teaspoon ground ginger

½ teaspoon ground cardamom

½ teaspoon ground nutmeg

¼ teaspoon ground cloves

¼ teaspoon freshly ground black pepper or white pepper

OATS

2 cups gluten-free or regular old-fashioned oats

3½ cups dairy-free milk or milk of choice

¼ cup chia seeds (optional; if not using, reduce milk by ½ cup)

3 tablespoons honey or maple syrup

1 tablespoon pure vanilla extract

½ teaspoon kosher salt

2 cups fresh berries, such as raspberries, blueberries, or blackberries, divided (It's more fun to pick your own, but in a pinch any berries will do.)

**Make the Berry Sauce**  In a small saucepan, stir together the berries, honey, salt, and zest. Bring to a strong simmer over medium heat, then cover, reduce heat to low, and continue cooking for 8 to 10 minutes, until the berries break down and the sauce thickens slightly. Remove from the heat and set aside.

**Make the Chai Spice Blend**  In a small bowl, whisk together the cinnamon, ginger, cardamom, nutmeg, cloves, and ginger and set aside.

**Make the Oat Mixture**  In a medium bowl, stir together the oats, milk, chia seeds (if using), honey, vanilla, and salt. Add 1 tablespoon plus 2 teaspoons of the chai spice blend, storing the rest in an airtight container for later use. Mix well to combine.

**Divide and Refrigerate**  Fill four (16-ounce) mason jars with 2 tablespoons of the berry sauce followed by ½ cup of the oat mixture. *Special Note: Continue to stir the oat mixture in the larger bowl as you go to ensure an even milk-to-oat ratio in each jar.*

Add ¼ cup of the fresh berries and 2 tablespoons of the berry sauce to each jar. Then divide the remaining oat mixture evenly among the four jars. Cover with lids and refrigerate overnight or for up to 2 days. If you don't have mason jars, a) you're missing out, and b) you can use any cups that are approximately 16 ounces in size and cover with plastic wrap overnight.

**Let's Eat!**  Remove the oats from the refrigerator and top with the remaining 1 cup fresh berries, dividing them equally among the four mason jars. Enjoy the fruits of your u-pick labor and savor the flavors of summer!

## Freestyle

Who said breakfast can't be a simple way to let the true you shine through? Customize your overnight oats with whatever toppings fuel your fire. I love adding shredded coconut, dark chocolate chips, or a dollop of homemade nut butter from my Sweet Potato Coins with Cashew and Pecan Nut Butters recipe (page 62).

# I'm Nuts for Coins

I TEND TO COOK by craving, using my kitchen as a studio to create edible art. You never know what to expect when visiting my Third Coast kitchen, but it's quite likely you'll get a chance to taste something new and different, or a creative combination like sweet potatoes and nut butter!

This recipe originated in Chicago when I was desperately trying to find something for dessert that was lower in sugar—but I had always used store-bought almond or peanut butter. Spending time in a place like Harbor Country inspires you to slow your roll, cool those engines, and make time for the really important things in life . . . like dreamy, creamy, so-delicious-you'll-eat-it-with-a-spoon homemade nut butter. And with that, I present my favorite healthy sweet treat to enjoy morning, noon, or night!

# Sweet Potato Coins with Cashew and Pecan Nut Butters

**Ψ¶ 6–8** delicious servings    ⧖ **1 hr 30 min** start to finish

SPECIAL ITEMS NEEDED

Food processor or high-powered blender

---

CASHEW CURRY MAPLE NUT BUTTER

1 tablespoon maple syrup

1 tablespoon light or dark brown sugar

1 tablespoon cooking oil of choice

2 tablespoons yellow curry powder

½ teaspoon kosher salt (Reduce to ¼ teaspoon if the nuts are already salted.)

1½ cups unsalted cashews

MAPLE PECAN CHOCOLATE NUT BUTTER

1 tablespoon maple syrup

1 tablespoon light or dark brown sugar

1 tablespoon cooking oil of choice

1 teaspoon pure vanilla extract

½ teaspoon kosher salt (Reduce to ¼ teaspoon if the nuts are already salted.)

1¾ cups unsalted roasted pecans

1 tablespoon plus 1 teaspoon unsweetened cocoa powder

SWEET POTATO COINS

3 large, long sweet potatoes

1 tablespoon cooking oil of choice

1 teaspoon ground nutmeg

1 teaspoon ground cinnamon

1 teaspoon ground ginger

1 teaspoon kosher salt

FOR SERVING

⅓ cup semisweet chocolate chips

Maldon sea salt, for garnish

**Prep** Arrange racks on the top and bottom thirds of the oven. Preheat the oven to 325°F. Line four baking sheets with parchment paper or aluminum foil, brush liberally with oil, and set aside.

**For the Cashew Nut Butter** In a medium bowl, whisk together the maple syrup, brown sugar, oil, curry powder, and salt until combined. Add the cashews and toss well to evenly coat. Spread the nuts in a single layer on one of the prepared baking sheets and set aside.

**For the Pecan Nut Butter** In a medium bowl, whisk together the maple syrup, brown sugar, oil, vanilla, and salt until combined. Add the pecans and toss well to evenly coat. Spread the nuts in a single layer on the second prepared baking sheet and set aside.

**Roast** Roast the cashews and pecans for 20 minutes, until fragrant. Halfway through cooking, stir the nuts and swap the baking sheets to ensure even cooking. Remove from the oven and let cool completely.

**For the Sweet Potato Coins** Raise the oven temperature to 400°F. Peel and slice the sweet potatoes into ½-inch-thick coins. Place the coins on the two remaining prepared baking sheets, about ½ inch apart in a single layer. Brush the tops with the oil, then sprinkle with the nutmeg, cinnamon, ginger, and salt.

Bake the sweet potato coins for about 25 minutes, or until the edges are browned and the coins are fork tender. Remove from the oven and let cool for 5 minutes.

**Blend the Cashew Nut Butter** While the potatoes cook, transfer the cashews to the bowl of a food processor or high-powered blender and blend until smooth, about 5 to 6 minutes, scraping down the sides as needed.

**Blend the Pecan Nut Butter** Transfer the pecans to the bowl of a clean food processor or high-powered blender and blend until almost smooth, about 2 to 3 minutes, scraping down the sides as needed. Add the cocoa at this time and continue blending until combined and the butter is smooth. Note that pecan butter is naturally thinner than cashew butter.

**Store the Nut Butter** If not using immediately, store the cashew butter in an airtight container in the refrigerator for about 3 weeks. I like storing mine in mason jars because fashion meeting function is a delicious thing! Remove the nut butter from the refrigerator 15 minutes before enjoying to let it soften.

**Let's Eat!** Arrange the sweet potato coins on a serving tray. Top half of the bites with a small dollop of the cashew butter and the other half with a small dollop of the pecan butter. Sprinkle with the chocolate chips and a few flakes of Maldon sea salt. Enjoy while warm and wonder how this meant-to-be flavor combination of sweet potato and nut butter has flown under the radar for so long.

# Join the Kale Klub

M Y HUSBAND ISN'T one to have a plate full of meat but then eat the salad first. However, on one curiously different spring day, he did just that. A few weeks before closing on our New Buffalo home, we found ourselves at the first annual Great Lakes Surf & Turf fundraiser at Flagship Specialty Foods and Fish Market. Chef and owner Rachel Collins was grilling fresh sturgeon and Mangalitsa hog, local wine and craft beer were flowing, and we were treated to lively tunes from musicians from the **School of American Music**, the beneficiary of this event.

"You have to try this lettuce!" David exclaimed, waving a forkful in front of my mouth. I took a bewildered bite and quickly understood why he was devouring these greens. They had a silky texture and just-harvested flavor, unlike anything I'd ever tasted. Asking around, we discovered the salad was sourced from a local vertical farm—and that the owner of the farm, Milan, was sitting just a few tables over.

Introductions were made, and our minds and palates were blown when we were invited to tour the vertical farm a couple of weeks later. Imagine superior-tasting lettuce and kale, grown vertically indoors year-round, that uses about 90 percent less water than conventional outdoor farming does. Suffice it to say, that's the only lettuce and kale we bought for the rest of the summer!

I threw this salad together to get David to eat more kale by combining it with several of his favorite ingredients: dill, Cheddar goat cheese, crispy chickpeas, and red pepper flakes. The result was unexpectedly delicious. Rich nut oil pairs well with the fresh, bright fennel and shallot, and there is plenty of crunch in every bite.

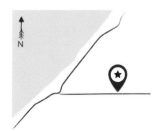

★ School of American Music

3 N. Elm St. | Three Oaks, MI

The School of American Music, located in the adorable Harbor Country town of Three Oaks, has grown to serve over 100 students since opening its doors in 2012. As a not-for-profit business, the school works to keep classes as affordable as possible, and the public can attend performances held twice a year.

# Unexpectedly Delicious Kale Salad

**4–6** refreshing servings    **25 min** start to finish

1 cup diced trimmed fennel bulb, fronds reserved, divided

3 tablespoons minced shallot

Zest of 1 lemon

2 tablespoons hazelnut, almond, pistachio, or walnut oil (I love La Tourangelle nut oils.)

1 tablespoon plus 2 teaspoons champagne vinegar or freshly squeezed lemon juice

1 teaspoon honey

½ teaspoon kosher salt, plus more to taste

¼ teaspoon freshly ground black pepper, plus more to taste

1 (5-ounce) box curly kale, thicker stems removed

½ cup shredded Cheddar goat cheese (I love Natural Valley Goat Cheese. In a pinch, use any sharp white Cheddar.)

2 tablespoons minced fresh dill, or 1 teaspoon dried dill

1 teaspoon red pepper flakes, plus more to taste (optional but awesome)

½ cup crispy chickpeas (I love Biena Chickpea Snacks, ranch or habañero! In a pinch, use nuts or seeds of choice to add a crunch.)

TIPS FOR SUCCESS

*Unlike me, this salad doesn't like to be overdressed. Spend a little extra time massaging the dressing into the kale, let it rest for 5 minutes, and then taste to decide if you want to add more.*

**Prep the Dressing and Vegetables**  Add the fennel, shallot, lemon zest, nut oil, vinegar, honey, salt, and pepper to a large salad bowl and toss well to combine the ingredients and coat the vegetables evenly.

**Prep the Kale**  Tear the kale into pieces about 2 inches long and add to the bowl. Mince 2 tablespoons (plus more for garnish) of the reserved fennel fronds.

**Finish the Salad**  Sprinkle the goat cheese, fennel fronds, dill, red pepper flakes (if using), and chickpeas over the kale, then use clean hands, salad tongs, or a large spoon and fork to gently mix together the salad. Ensure the kale is evenly coated. Add salt and pepper to taste.

**Let's Eat!**  Chill salad bowls or plates in the freezer for 10 to 15 minutes before serving. Plate the salad and garnish with some fresh fennel fronds before serving.

# Zoodle Is the New Noodle

I'M NOT GOING to frosting coat this, kids. Years ago, when I found out my then-boyfriend David was dairy- and gluten-intolerant, it was like my entire kitchen was cast in this odd shade of gray. I felt confused, disappointed, and even betrayed! I had won his heart by cooking plentiful pasta dishes and baking countless cookies and cakes. And we loved eating ice cream together!

At the time, options for gluten- and dairy-free products were very limited. So, for several months, I sulked. Eventually I realized my future hubby was still hungry for my home cooking, so I dusted off my standing mixer, ironed my apron, and began experimenting with how to remove the gluten and dairy from a few of his favorite recipes!

The original version of this recipe is made with regular gluten-free spaghetti, but during our first summer in Harbor Country we made an effort to eat healthier, lighter meals so we could paddleboard faster and cycle longer. Enter fresh zucchini and a spiralizer.

I'm not a fan of pine nuts, so I swapped them for pepitas—small pumpkin seeds without the shells found in certain pumpkin varieties. They are delicious, but hard to find sometimes, so in a pinch, any roasted shelled pumpkin seeds will work.

Pesto isn't pesto without the umami taste that typically comes from freshly grated Pecorino or Parmigiano-Reggiano cheese. In this dairy-free recipe, we can all thank nutritional yeast for delivering the savory flavor. David was a little concerned about the unfamiliar ingredient, but the pesto zoodles got the hubby stamp of approval after his first bite!

★ **Granor Farm**

3480 Warren Woods Rd. | Three Oaks, MI

In July and August, Harbor Country is bursting with its very best zucchini. I like to pick mine up at Granor Farm, where everything is organic and bursting with the very best flavors Mother Nature has to offer.

# Pepita Pesto Zoodle Noodle Salad

🍴 **4–6** refreshing servings  ⏳ **30 min** start to finish

SPECIAL ITEMS NEEDED

Food processor or blender

Spiralizer tool or mandoline with julienne blade

---

PESTO SAUCE

1½ cups stemmed and loosely packed fresh basil leaves

2 cups stemmed and loosely packed fresh baby spinach leaves

¼ cup roasted pepitas (In a pinch, use any shelled pumpkin seeds.)

1 clove garlic, peeled

6 tablespoons olive oil

3 tablespoons freshly squeezed lemon juice

2 tablespoons nutritional yeast (found at many markets in the health food section)

¾ teaspoon kosher salt

½ teaspoon honey or agave (In a pinch, use granulated sugar.)

½ teaspoon freshly ground black pepper

ZUCCHINI NOODLES

4 large zucchini

GARNISH

Lemon zest

Fresh basil leaves

Pepitas

**Make the Pesto Sauce**  Combine all the ingredients for the sauce, starting with the basil and ending with the pepper, in a blender or food processor fit with the blade attachment. Pulse until well combined but not completely smooth, about 1 minute.

**Make the Zucchini Noodles**  Cut off the ends of the zucchini. Use a spiralizer tool or mandoline with a julienne blade to make zucchini noodles about the size of spaghetti.

**Let's Eat!**  Place the zucchini noodles in a medium bowl and drizzle about ½ cup of the pesto over the top. Use a large spoon and fork or tongs to gently toss to coat. Sample a bite and decide if you'd like to add more pesto. Garnish with the lemon zest, fresh basil leaves, and pepitas. Enjoy immediately, or store covered in the refrigerator for up to 2 days. If you store, zucchini contains a good amount of water—so make sure to drain any excess liquid before serving.

The remaining pesto can be stored in an airtight jar in the refrigerator for 3 to 5 days or frozen for up to 1 month.

# Crunch and Spice, Oh So Nice

The warmer weather arrived at a sloth-slow pace during our first spring in Harbor Country, but I noticed that the crocus flowers must have missed the memo to stay underground for a few more weeks. As I shivered and shuffled along on a morning run in late March, inch-tall pops of purple sprung from the earth, reminding me that warmer days were in fact just around the bend.

After a long, hot post-run shower that returned feeling to my tingling toes, I headed off to **Barney's Market** in search of some inspiration for dinner. There I saw another sign that spring had indeed sprung, at least somewhere in the United States. The thin, stringy asparagus of winter had been replaced by thick, steakhouse-worthy spears. I grabbed several vibrant bundles.

Back at home we enjoyed the springtime vegetable in a matter of minutes. This super swift preparation pairs the light, bright flavors of lemon and jalapeño with rich nut oil and roasted pecans, perfect for transitioning the palate out of winter and back into the warm summer sun.

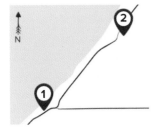

**1 Barney's Market**

10 N. Thompson St. | New Buffalo, MI

**2 Sawyer Home and Garden Center**

5865 Sawyer Rd. | Sawyer, MI

In Harbor Country, asparagus season runs April through June. Bundles of locally grown, bright green stalks fill the grocery stores, like Barney's Market, and farmers markets alike. I also love visiting Sawyer Home and Garden Center in peak season for some of the best asparagus Southwest Michigan has to offer.

# Roasted Jalapeño Pecan Asparagus with Lemon Zest

🍴 **4–6** simply refreshing servings  ⏳ **30 min** start to finish

1 medium jalapeño

2 bundles asparagus spears (about 35 spears, ½ inch wide and 10 inches long)

3 tablespoons almond, walnut, hazelnut, or pistachio nut oil, divided (I love La Tourangelle nut oils.)

2 teaspoons coconut sugar or sugar of choice

½ cup chopped unsalted pecans or nuts of choice (If using salted nuts, reduce salt by half.)

Zest of 2 lemons

¾ teaspoon kosher salt, plus more to taste

Freshly ground black pepper, to taste

TIPS FOR SUCCESS
*Make sure the asparagus is very dry before roasting to avoid steaming. Select thicker asparagus for a more tender texture.*

**Prep**  Preheat the oven to 400°F (on the roast setting, if you have one). Line one to two baking sheets (depending on size) with aluminum foil or parchment paper and brush with oil. Set aside. (If you arrange the asparagus in two rows going across the short end of the baking sheet, they should fit on one sheet.)

**Cut the Jalapeño**  Cut off the jalapeño stem and discard. Slice the jalapeño in half lengthwise and use a spoon to scrape out the seeds. Slice crosswise into thin pieces and set aside.

**Roast**  Pat the asparagus dry with paper towels. Chop off the tougher white ends. Place the asparagus in an even layer on the prepared baking sheet(s). (If using two baking sheets, divide all the ingredients between them evenly.) Drizzle the asparagus with 2 tablespoons of the nut oil and sprinkle with the sugar. Using clean hands or tongs, toss to coat the asparagus, then rearrange it in a single layer. Scatter the jalapeño slices, pecan pieces, and lemon zest evenly over the asparagus. Roast for 6 to 10 minutes, depending on the thickness of the asparagus spears, until fork tender. (Resist overcooking, as they can become too soft.)

**Let's Eat!**  Transfer the asparagus to a serving platter or plates. Drizzle with the remaining 1 tablespoon of nut oil, sprinkle with the salt and pepper, and toss to coat. This crazy-versatile dish can be served room temperature as part of a picnic spread, as an appetizer (especially if you cut asparagus into 3-inch bites), or hot as a side dish to an entrée such as the Beet-Red Sunset Salmon with Miso, Maple, and Roasted Fennel (page 22).

# Adding Flare to Fall Fare

A S OUR FIRST fall approached in Harbor Country, I wasn't ready to say goodbye to the three delicious months that had felt like adult summer camp, ripe with long beach days, sunset paddles, and warm, breezy dinners on the screened porch.

Determined to squeeze in a few more bike rides before the snow fell, I jumped on my bike with a basket and rode the nine miles out to Dinges' Fall Harvest. There I grabbed two large butternut beauties, thanked owner Lee Dinges kindly for selling them to me past 6 p.m., and cycled another nine miles home, wobbling a bit from the extra 10 pounds of squash on board but happy as any October birthday girl could be.

I have converted an unusual number of people from brussels sprout haters into brussels sprout lovers, all thanks to this very recipe, which combines golden butternut squash, caramelized brussels sprouts, sweet-tart cherries, and toasted pecans. Now it's time for you to try your hand at making this roasted crowd-pleasing recipe. And who knows? You might just get a few hesitant friends to climb aboard the brussels sprout bandwagon!

# Brown Sugar Chili Brussels Sprouts with Butternut Squash and Cherries

🍴 **8–10** craveable servings   🕐 **30 min** active time   ⏳ **1 hr 15 min** start to finish

2 pounds brussels sprouts, ends trimmed and halved lengthwise

2 large butternut squash, peeled, seeded, and cut into 1-inch cubes about the same size as each brussels sprout (about 6 cups)

¼ cup olive oil

½ cup light or dark brown sugar

2 tablespoons mild or hot chili powder

1 tablespoon kosher salt, plus more to taste

2 teaspoons freshly ground black pepper, or 1 teaspoon red pepper flakes, plus more to taste

2 teaspoons ground allspice (optional)

1⅓ cups dried cherries, coarsely chopped

1½ cups pecans, coarsely chopped

TIPS FOR SUCCESS

*If using whole butternut squash, choose large squash with longer tops and smaller bulbs, which is where the seeds are found. It's far easier to cut cubes from the longer solid portion of the squash.*

**Prep**  Preheat the oven to 400°F. Line two baking sheets with parchment paper or aluminum foil, brush with oil, and set aside.

**Dress the Brussels Sprouts and Butternut Squash**  In a large mixing bowl, mix together the brussels sprouts and squash. Drizzle with the olive oil, sprinkle the brown sugar evenly over the top, and add the chili powder, salt, pepper, and allspice (if using). Toss using a spatula or two large spoons, ensuring the vegetables are evenly coated. Add more salt and pepper to taste.

**Roast**  Divide the vegetable medley evenly between the two prepared baking sheets in one layer to avoid steaming. Roast in the oven for 25 to 30 minutes. Remove the baking sheets from the oven and evenly divide the cherries and pecans between them, sprinkling over the vegetables. Use a spatula to gently toss the cherries and pecans with the vegetables before returning to the oven to roast another 10 to 15 minutes, until the brussels sprouts and squash are fork tender and the edges have browned.

**Let's Eat!**  Fill a large serving dish with the roasted vegetable medley. If not serving immediately, keep warm until you're ready to bestow this craveable side dish upon your guests, who are likely to start requesting that you make this for most holidays and other days.

## Freestyle

Replace the olive oil with your favorite nut oil or coconut oil.

Sprinkle with 8 ounces of soft crumbled goat cheese or crumbled blue cheese before serving.

Replace the dried cherries with chopped dried fruit of your choice.

# Picnic Perfect

Harbor Country is a place made for picnics! Whether you're at the beach, in an apple orchard, at a vineyard, or simply on your own front lawn, summer and fall provide the ideal weather for eating alfresco!

What makes picnic-perfect fare? For my family, it needs to taste great at room temperature and travel well in a cooler or picnic basket.

These recipes are some of my favorites in the book because they celebrate the most delicious time of year in Southwest Michigan. Tiffy's Summertime Key Lime Butter Cookies (page 100) are ridiculously addictive and easy to make, and the Crispy Golden Oven-Baked Fried Chicken with Chile Honey Drizzle (page 84) just might make all your picnic dreams come true.

As you picnic your way through Harbor Country, check out some of the local places mentioned in this chapter, such as Kaminksi Farms (for fresh chicken), Hansing's Happy Hens (for duck eggs), and Luisa's Café and Harbert Swedish Bakery (for excellent sandwich bread).

Life's short . . . plan less, picnic more!

# Oven Bake for Goodness' Sake

GROWING UP IN Lake Tahoe, the Fourth of July wasn't complete without eating my mom's oven-baked fried chicken while we were bundled in beach towels on our boat and watching the fireworks.

While writing this book, I learned that my mom actually smuggled the recipe for this deliciously crispy chicken to the West Coast from her mom's Madison, Wisconsin, kitchen. I love knowing that Grandma Willo, ever the trailblazer, was making a healthier version of fried chicken even back in the 1950s!

Once I had my own kitchen, I started making versions of this childhood chicken. However, I never asked my mom to hand over the actual recipe until this cookbook project. But, like most of the fabulous food that comes out of her kitchen, there was no recipe. She made it from memory, a little different from the way my grandma did and using whatever she had on hand at the time. There were just two constants: crispy-crunchy and full of flavor.

So, with the taste memory from my Tahoe days in mind, I set out to make a version of the oven-baked fried chicken that would make both my grandma and my mamma proud, while granting hubby's request for "extra crunch please!" After several days of recipe testing, we finally have a written family recipe for Midwest-made, oven-baked fried chicken!

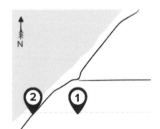

### 1 Black Bull Fireworks
10505 US-12 | Michigan City, IN

### 2 Krazy Kaplans Fireworks
10351 IN-39 | La Porte, IN

In Harbor Country, it's easy to catch multiple firework displays over the holiday weekend across all the tiny lakeside towns. David was quick to latch on to the local tradition of buying fireworks and lighting them off at the beach on the Fourth of July and throughout the summer. We like to buy fireworks at Black Bull Fireworks, located between Michigan City and New Buffalo. We also like Krazy Kaplans Fireworks, which has four locations between Chicago and New Buffalo. If you decide to join in the DIY firework shows, just check on the local township rules, as they vary from place to place.

# Crispy Golden Oven-Baked Fried Chicken with Chile Honey Drizzle

🍴 **8–10** crispy-licious servings   🕐 **45 min** active time   ⧖ **1 hr 40 min** start to finish

## CHICKEN "BUTTERMILK" MARINADE

3 cups almond milk or milk of choice, plus more as needed

2 tablespoons freshly squeezed lemon juice

16 pieces of chicken legs and/or thighs, bone-in or boneless

## SPICED FLOUR COATING

1½ cups gluten-free all-purpose flour *without* xanthan gum or regular all-purpose flour

1½ cups gluten-free or regular panko crumbs

¼ cup cornmeal

2 tablespoons dried chives

2 teaspoons dried basil

2 teaspoons paprika

2 teaspoons onion powder

1¼ teaspoons ground white pepper

1 teaspoon poultry seasoning

1 teaspoon granulated sugar

1 teaspoon baking powder

¾ teaspoon kosher salt

½ teaspoon celery salt

½ teaspoon freshly ground black pepper

½ teaspoon dried mustard

½ teaspoon ground cayenne pepper (optional)

¼ teaspoon ground nutmeg (optional)

¾ cup (1½ sticks) plus 4 tablespoons salted butter, melted and divided

## CHILE HONEY

⅓ cup honey

½ teaspoon red pepper flakes

**Make the Chicken "Buttermilk" Marinade and Soak the Chicken** In a large bowl, whisk together the almond milk and lemon juice. Let sit for 5 minutes. Add the chicken pieces to the bowl with the milk mixture. The milk should just cover the chicken, so add a bit more if needed. Let sit at room temperature for 30 minutes.

**Prep** Line two baking sheets with parchment paper or aluminum foil. Set aside.

**Preheat the Baking Dishes** Place 2 (9 × 13-inch) baking dishes on the middle rack and preheat the oven to 450°F. Preheating the baking dishes makes the chicken extra crispy! (Oven-safe glass or ceramic baking dishes work best.)

**Make the Spiced Flour Coating** In a medium bowl, whisk together the flour, panko, cornmeal, chives, basil, paprika, onion powder, white pepper, poultry seasoning, sugar, baking powder, kosher salt, celery salt, black pepper, dried mustard, cayenne pepper (if using), and nutmeg (if using).

**Coat the Chicken** Arrange the chicken marinade bowl, flour mixture bowl, and prepared baking sheets in a row. To dredge easily, you need one "wet hand" and one "dry hand." I use my left hand (wet) to pull the chicken from the milk and drop it into the flour, then my right hand (dry) to cover the chicken in the flour blend with a large spoon and place it on the baking sheet. Repeat until all the chicken is coated.

**Oven Fry** Remove the baking dishes from the oven and brush with ¾ cup of the melted butter. Divide the chicken evenly between the dishes, arranging the pieces in a single layer, at least ½ inch apart. *Special Note: If using a mix of chicken, place all the boneless pieces in one dish and the bone-in pieces in another due to the different baking times required for each.* Drizzle 2 tablespoons of the melted butter evenly over the chicken in each dish. Return the dishes to the oven. Place the bone-in chicken on the upper rack (hotter) and the boneless chicken on the lower rack (cooler).

*Special Note: For boneless, skinless thighs, bake for 20 to 25 minutes total. For skin-on, bone-in chicken legs or thighs, bake for 30 to 35 minutes total. The internal temperature for both the boneless and bone-in chicken should reach 165°F.*

Halfway through the baking time, remove the chicken from the oven and *very* carefully flip each piece using a spatula and fork to ensure the crust stays intact. Drizzle the chicken evenly with the remaining 2 tablespoons melted butter. Return to the oven and continue baking until crispy and golden brown. Remove from the oven and let rest 10 minutes before serving.

**Make the Chile Honey** While the chicken rests, in a small bowl, stir together the honey and red pepper flakes.

**Let's Eat!** Serve the chile honey with the chicken for drizzling. Store leftover chicken in the refrigerator, covered, for 3 to 4 days. Enjoy hot or at room temperature.

TIPS FOR SUCCESS
*Using three baking dishes for this quantity of chicken will allow you to bake it all at one time. If you only have two baking dishes that are smaller than 9 × 13 inches, bake in two batches to avoid overcrowding and steaming the chicken.*

# Who Leeked the Recipe?

THERE ARE TWO things I've seen more of in Harbor Country than anywhere else: corn and goat cheese. Seeing the endless fields of corn as I cycled through the countryside didn't exactly come as a surprise given that we're in the Midwest, but the unusually wide variety of goat cheese definitely caught my attention.

Given David's cow dairy allergy and his lovely gluten sensitivity, he was beyond thrilled to unearth a treasure trove of different cheeses made with goat milk at both local grocery stores like Barney's Market and seasonal farmers markets in the area (like **New Buffalo Farmers Market** and **Skip's New Buffalo European Farmers Market**). Everything from mozzarella and Cheddar to muenster and colby jack is available for the goat cheese lover in you! (Many people—but not all—who can't eat cow milk are actually fine with goat or sheep milk. Best to double-check with your dairy-free guests.)

So what's a girl to do with easy access to fields of fresh sweet corn and mountains of locally made goat cheese? You know the drill! Into the kitchen I go to do a little matchmaking, and voilà! Out of the oven pop these tender, savory corn muffins, filled with leeks because they're lovely, and brimming with Cheddar goat cheese. And because muffins look suspiciously like cupcakes, I top them with a savory goat cheese "frosting." I hope your family devours these portable picnic snacks as quickly as we did all summer long!

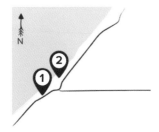

**1 New Buffalo Farmers Market**

910 W. Buffalo St. | New Buffalo, MI

**2 Skip's New Buffalo European Farmers Market**

16710 Lakeshore Rd. | New Buffalo, MI

Looking for local cheeses in Harbor Country? Head to New Buffalo Farmers Market, held Thursdays starting at 4 p.m. in downtown New Buffalo. Skip's New Buffalo European Farmers Market, held Saturdays and Sundays from 9 a.m. to 3 p.m. on Red Arrow Highway, also has a great selection of artisan cheeses.

# Cornbread Leek Muffins with Chipotle Goat Cheese "Frosting"

🍴 **12–15** delicious servings   🕐 **40 min** active time   ⏳ **1 hr** start to finish

CORNBREAD LEEK MUFFINS

2 medium leeks

2 tablespoons salted
butter or olive oil

1 cup gluten-free all-purpose
flour *with* xanthan gum or regular
all-purpose flour (I use Cup4Cup
Multipurpose Flour or Bob's
Red Mill 1 to 1 Baking Flour. )

1 cup cornmeal

⅓ cup firmly packed
light brown sugar

½ teaspoon baking soda

¼ teaspoon baking powder

½ teaspoon ground white
pepper (In a pinch, use freshly
ground black pepper.)

½ teaspoon kosher salt

2 eggs

1 cup dairy-free milk
or milk of choice

½ cup (1 stick) salted butter,
melted and cooled slightly

2 cups shredded Cheddar goat
cheese or Cheddar of choice

CHIPOTLE GOAT CHEESE
"FROSTING"

½ cup goat cheese or vegan
or regular cream cheese

½ cup minced fresh chives
or green onions

1½ teaspoons ground chipotle
pepper (In a pinch, use chili
powder or paprika.)

2 teaspoons honey

¼ teaspoon kosher salt

¼ teaspoon freshly
ground black pepper

**Prep**  Brush a 12-cup muffin tin with oil. This method of baking without paper liners gives the edges a cheesy, buttery crunch, which ups the yum factor! Preheat the oven to 350°F.

**Dice and Sauté the Leeks**  Cut off the root ends and the tough, darker green top portions (which you can discard or save to make stock) of the leeks. Peel away any damaged layers from the white parts of the leeks. Slice the round white portions of the leeks into 4 quarters lengthwise, then dice crosswise into small pieces. You should have about 1¾ cups of diced leek pieces. Place in a mesh strainer and rinse to remove any dirt. Pat dry with a paper towel and set aside.

In a medium skillet over medium-high heat, melt the butter for about 1 minute. Add the leeks and sauté, stirring often and reducing the heat as needed to prevent burning, until tender, 5 to 6 minutes. Remove from the heat and set aside.

**Prepare the Batter**  In a large bowl, whisk together the flour, cornmeal, brown sugar, baking soda, baking powder, pepper, and salt until thoroughly combined. Set aside.

In a medium bowl, whisk together the eggs and milk until combined. Whisk in the cooled melted butter. Add the milk mixture to the flour mixture and stir with a wooden spoon until just combined, scraping down the sides of the bowl with a spatula as needed. Your batter should be a little lumpy. Use a spatula to gently fold in the shredded cheese and leeks.

Use a ¼-cup measure or medium ice cream scoop to fill each muffin tin cup two-thirds full. Bake for 18 to 22 minutes, until the tops are slightly golden and a toothpick inserted into the center of one of the muffins comes out clean. Remove and let cool for about 10 minutes before removing from the tin.

**Make the Chipotle Goat Cheese "Frosting"**  While the muffins bake, make the frosting. Put the goat cheese in a small microwave-safe bowl and microwave at 30-second intervals until soft enough to easily spread. This should take 30 to 60 seconds. Add the chives, chipotle pepper, honey, salt, and black pepper. Whip together with a fork until smooth and combined.

**Let's Eat!**  These muffins are fantastic when eaten fresh from the oven with a generous dollop of savory frosting. Store extras refrigerated in an airtight container. Reheat by wrapping in aluminum foil and placing in a 350°F oven until warm, or microwaving for 15 to 30 seconds.

# Can You Feel the Bries?

I LOVE NEW. There's excitement, energy, and adventure in new. One of the best parts of our first year in Harbor Country was all the new people we met, like the father-son duo Milan and Dan, who own a local vertical farm.

We invited these innovative farmers over one evening for happy hour at Camp Navama. They arrived with sparkling wine, some of their legendary vertically grown basil leaves (as large as my palm!), and a small wheel of goat milk Brie from Sawyer Home and Garden Center—a curiously addictive place that sells everything from plants and outdoor grills to gourmet groceries, gifts, and holiday decor.

Milan asked for a knife and cutting board and swiftly whipped up what has become one of my go-to appetizers all year long. I've added a variety of fun flavor combinations you can try out, but don't be afraid to open your pantry and let your taste buds guide you to create your signature version of this versatile happy hour hors d'oeuvre.

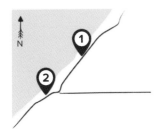

**1 Hearthwoods Custom Furnishings**  **2 The Villager**

15310 Red Arrow Hwy. | Lakeside, MI     100 N. Whittaker St. | New Buffalo, MI

If you need a new serving tray for these basil-Brie beauties, stop by Hearthwoods in Lakeside. The Villager in New Buffalo also has a great selection of home decor and gifts. Both stores are well worth a visit when in Harbor Country.

TRIPLE CRÈME
Goat Brie
Rich and Creamy Soft Ripened
Goat's Milk Cheese
Net Wt. 6.5 oz. (180 g)
Keep Refrigerated

Woolwich Dairy Inc.
Est. 1983

# New Buffalo Basil-Wrapped Goat Milk Brie Cheese

**4–6** indulgent servings    **20 min** start to finish

1 (6½-ounce) wheel goat milk Brie cheese (Often locally available at Sawyer Home and Garden Center. In a pinch, use cow or sheep milk Brie.)

1 (3-ounce) package fresh basil

Jam

Nuts

Honey

Balsamic glaze

Sun-dried tomatoes

TIPS FOR SUCCESS
*Cut the cheese while it is still chilled from the refrigerator, which makes it easier to slice. Let soften slightly in basil wraps before serving.*

**Prep the Cheese and Basil**  Remove the Brie wheel from the refrigerator and use a sharp knife to slice the wheel into ⅓-inch-thick strips. Cut any longer strips in half so they are about 2 inches in length. Remove any stems from the basil leaves.

**Put These Babies Together!**  To assemble, place 1 slice of the Brie horizontally at the narrow end of a larger basil leaf. Top the cheese with preferred ingredient options, then roll the basil around the cheese and secure with a toothpick.

**Let's Eat!**  Serve on your favorite party tray.

## Freestyle

These are my preferred combinations, but you can combine whatever flavors you like.

Local Fruit Jam + Pecans

Sun-Dried Tomatoes + Balsamic Glaze

Local Michigan Honey + Pistachios

# Quack Over Cluck

IT WAS A sunny summer Saturday at **Skip's New Buffalo European Farmers Market** when David discovered duck eggs for the very first time.

"These are duck eggs!" he called excitedly from the Hansing's Happy Hens stall. "They're huge and have more protein than regular eggs," he said, hard selling me. "We'll take two dozen," he said to the vendor.

"We'll take one dozen," I intercepted, "to try them out."

"We'll love them," he insisted. "We'll stick with the two dozen."

Duck eggs weren't the only things David had learned to love during our first Harbor Country summer. His feelings about egg salad (previously a food he'd never consider eating) also took a turn for the better thanks to a delicious version Whistle Stop Grocery makes that somehow tempted his taste buds.

Armed with 24 duck eggs, I set out to make an epic duck egg salad recipe. In our family, that means it's easy on the mayo and packed with flavor and plenty of crunch. After a few trials I found that radish and fennel were a refreshing substitute for celery to cut through the rich yolks. Pepitas added a savory crunch, and chipotle gave just the right amount of heat. I typically serve it on toasted local bread from Luisa's Café and Harbert Swedish Bakery or Skip's, or on Schär Gluten Free Deli Style Bread Seeded from Barney's Market. My paleo people love it over fresh salad. The next time you're craving an egg salad sandwich, give duck eggs a whirl. They really are all they're quacked up to be!

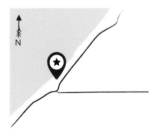

★ **Skip's New Buffalo European Farmers Market**

16710 Lakeshore Rd. | New Buffalo, MI

Hansing's Happy Hens is a local company that provides the community with delicious, organic, allergy-friendly duck eggs. (Some people who can't eat chicken eggs can eat duck eggs.) The happy hens are never caged but instead live the good life in a barn and outdoors, enjoying a natural diet mostly made up of grass and bugs. In the summer and early fall, the duck eggs can be found at various local farmers markets such as Skip's.

# Golden Duck Egg Salad with Radish, Pepitas, and Fennel

**🍴 6–8** picnic-perfect servings   **⏳ 1 hr** start to finish

12 duck eggs

6 tablespoons favorite mayonnaise (I love Sir Kensington's Chipotle Fabanaise.)

¼ cup sweet pickle relish

3 tablespoons plain yellow or stone-ground mustard

1 tablespoon white wine or champagne vinegar

1 cup finely chopped trimmed fennel bulb, fronds reserved, divided

½ cup finely diced shallot (About 2 medium shallots; in a pinch, use red or white onion.)

½ cup finely chopped radish

1 teaspoon kosher salt, plus more to taste

½ teaspoon ground turmeric (optional)

½ teaspoon red pepper flakes (optional)

¼ teaspoon freshly ground black pepper, plus more to taste

⅓ cup roasted pepitas (In a pinch, use any shelled pumpkin seeds.)

**Boil the Eggs**  Place the eggs in a large soup pot and fill the pot with cold water until the eggs are fully covered. Over high heat, bring to a rolling boil. Once boiling, remove from the heat and let stand for 13 minutes. Immediately drain the hot water, then shake the pot in a circular motion to crack the egg-shells a bit. Refill the pot with cold water to cover the eggs, let stand for about 1 minute, then drain and refill a second time with enough cold water to cover the eggs. This stops them from overcooking. Add 4 cups of ice to the pot. Cool completely, about 15 minutes.

**Peel the Eggs**  Once the eggs are cooled, drain the water, remove the eggs, and refill the pot with cool water one last time. Peel the eggs over the water, dipping them under as needed to remove the shells. To peel, pinch the bottom of the egg to remove that portion of the shell, tapping on a hard surface if needed. Gently squeeze the eggshell with your fingers anywhere it still needs to be shattered. Going from the bottom up, work your thumb gently between the thin, skin-like membrane of the egg and the egg white itself. Once you are able to get under the skin of the egg, the whole shell will easily peel away in large pieces. Sometimes 1 or 2 eggs in the dozen are harder to peel and may not peel perfectly, but not to worry. They're about to be mashed anyway!

**Make the Salad**  On a large cutting board, cut each egg in half lengthwise, place them flat side down, then medium chop into square-ish pieces. Place the chopped eggs in a large mixing bowl. Add the mayonnaise, pickle relish, mustard, and vinegar, tossing gently with a spatula or large spoon to coat. Use two knives to chop up the eggs in the bowl a bit more. Mince ¼ cup of the reserved fennel fronds. Add the chopped fennel, shallot, radish, salt, turmeric (if using), red pepper flakes (if using), pepper, and pepitas.

Using a large fork, stir to combine all the ingredients, smashing the eggs a little as you go until the desired consistency is reached.

**Let's Eat!**  The beauty of this luxuriously rich duck egg salad is that it's a crowd-pleaser! For the sandwich lover in your life who still considers bread a friend, lightly toast 2 slices of really delicious local bread. Spread with a generous layer of duck egg salad on one side and cover with the other. Then slice in half. For anyone wanting to have their duck egg salad and green salad too, serve it atop a fresh bed of local lettuce, dressed lightly with olive oil, lemon juice, and a sprinkle of salt and pepper.

# Key Limes Offer Good Times

Have you ever found a favorite "lost" recipe? Maybe it's one from your childhood that your secretive grandmother finally decided to hand over, or a roast chicken recipe from *Bon Appétit* magazine that you used to win over many unsuspecting hearts but got lost in the move from L.A. to Chicago. Whatever the case, when you get to revisit a winning recipe from the past, it's pure magic.

For me it was my Key Lime Butter Cookies recipe that I'd developed in my early 20s when I started a gourmet cookie company after college. During the recipe-testing phase, Tiffany, my best friend from high school, was more than happy to sit on my kitchen counter "helping me with recipe development" by tasting the dough and eating cookies for lunch. The Key Lime Butter Cookies were her favorite by far and became my best seller. But when I finally decided to close the company after several years, I had zero interest in baking cookies for the foreseeable future.

During our first summer in Harbor Country, Tiffany was pregnant with her first baby. I flew out to Reno, Nevada, for her baby shower, and she asked me to make the Key Lime Butter Cookies for the party. After baking one tart, buttery batch, I couldn't wait to add this recipe to my New Buffalo dessert rotation.

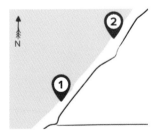

**1 Townline Beach**

10379 Townline Rd. | Union Pier, MI

**2 Warren Dunes State Park**

12032 Red Arrow Hwy. | Sawyer, MI

These buttery, bite-size cookies are the perfect summertime treat to pack for a relaxing day at one of Harbor Country's many beaches. One of my favorite local public beaches is Townline Beach in Union Pier (which has decent parking and tends to get fewer crowds in the summer than other public beaches nearby). Warren Dunes State Park has an expansive stretch of pure white sand and large dunes to hike. Head to one of these beaches to work up your appetite for Tiffy's Summertime Key Lime Butter Cookies!

# Tiffy's Summertime Key Lime Butter Cookies

🍴 **24–30** soft, tart, buttery cookies  🕐 **45 min** active time  ⧖ **2 hrs** start to finish

BUTTER COOKIES

1 cup (2 sticks) salted
butter, softened

1 cup granulated sugar

1 egg yolk

½ teaspoon pure vanilla extract

2 teaspoons real Key lime juice
(I love Nellie & Joe's, often
available at Barney's Market.)

¼ teaspoon sea salt

1¾ cups all-purpose gluten-
free flour *with* xanthan gum or
regular all-purpose flour (I use
Cup4Cup Multipurpose Flour.)

KEY LIME ICING

1¾ cups confectioners' sugar

2 tablespoons real Key lime juice

1 teaspoon pure vanilla extract

⅛ teaspoon sea salt

Green food coloring (optional)

TIPS FOR SUCCESS

*Don't overmix the dough or it will
become tough. Package these up
for a delicious host gift!*

**Prep**  Preheat the oven to 350°F and line two baking sheets with parchment paper or aluminum foil. Brush lightly with oil and set aside.

**Make the Dough**  In a medium bowl using a whisk, an electric handheld mixer, or a standing mixer fit with the paddle attachment, cream together the butter and sugar until light and fluffy, about 2 minutes on medium speed, scraping the sides of the bowl with a spatula as needed. Pause the mixer and add the egg yolk, vanilla, Key lime juice, and salt, and then mix on medium speed until just combined. Pause the mixer to add the flour and, moving from low to medium speed, mix until just combined.

**Bake and Cool**  Using a small ice cream scoop (about 1-inch diameter) or a tablespoon, drop the dough in balls about 2 inches apart on the prepared baking sheets. Briefly roll each scoop between your palms to form more perfect balls. *Special Note: If you prefer a slightly thicker, chewier cookie, refrigerate the dough balls for 10 minutes before baking.* Bake at 350°F for 10 to 12 minutes, until the edges are slightly golden and lift up easily with a spatula. Once done, leave on the baking sheets to cool completely, 30 to 45 minutes. Cool them more quickly by putting them in the refrigerator for about 20 minutes or the freezer for 15 minutes.

**Make the Vanilla Key Lime Icing**  While the cookies cool, make the icing. In the bowl of a standing mixer fit with the paddle attachment (or using a hand mixer in a medium bowl), add the confectioners' sugar and mix for about 1 minute to remove any lumps. Add the Key lime juice, vanilla, and salt. Mix on medium to medium-high speed until smooth. Add 1 to 2 drops of the green food coloring (if using), then mix for an even color. Add warm water as needed until you can easily drizzle the icing with a fork.

**Ice the Cookies**  Once the cookies are completely cooled, dip a fork into the icing and then drizzle it quickly and evenly back and forth over the cookies to make stripes. (Whisk the icing as needed if a layer of crust has formed.) Let the icing harden on the cookies for about 30 minutes before serving, or for 1 hour before storing.

**Let's Eat!**  These cookies will last in an airtight container for 4 to 5 days or in the freezer up to 1 month . . . but honestly, they tend to get eaten in about 24 hours because they're bite-size, buttery, and oh so craveable!

# Apple Cider Seeking Rider

"**H**I, WE'RE THE JOLLYS . . . AND WE ARE!" That was our first introduction to our New Buffalo neighbors, who have since become awesome friends. Thanks to the Jollys, David and I now know there's a difference between bike riding and cycling. The latter requires hours, not minutes, "in the saddle," serious leg strength, padded biking shorts—and the removal of any bells and kickstands, as we soon discovered.

Excited by the idea of becoming a legit cyclist in one summer, David took Mr. Fred Jolly up on his offer to "train" him (and eventually us) for the 100-mile **Apple Cider Century** ride, which begins in the cozy little town of Three Oaks, Michigan, and takes place every September. For the first ride, Navy man Fred showed up promptly at zero eight hundred hours. Off they rode toward the countryside, teacher and grasshopper, on the first of many cycling adventures.

David was ravenous when he got back, and I knew this super-serious cyclist would need to start eating a quick, carb-rich snack before his early morning rides. This was the perfect opportunity to create a delicious homemade bar that was also gluten-, nut-, and dairy-free and packed full of nutrients.

This hearty bar is filled with healthy oats and chia seeds, crunchy pumpkin seeds, sweet dried figs, a touch of chocolate, and of course apples, to honor the Apple Cider Century ride.

### ★ Apple Cider Century

Starts and ends at Three Oaks Elementary School (routes vary)
100 Oak St. | Three Oaks, MI

Since 1974, the Apple Cider Century ride, which draws over 5,500 participants each year, has grown to be the Midwest's largest one-day century ride. The routes change annually, always starting in Three Oaks and touring cyclists through the orchards, forests, and wine country of Southwest Michigan and Northwest Indiana. Participants can choose to ride 15, 25, 37, 50, 62, 75, or 100 miles, so it's a terrific event for families or more serious cyclists. And since it's not a race, there's plenty of time to stop at the refreshment stands to enjoy fresh-picked apples and apple cider.

# Apple Cider Rider Bar

**12–16** super-snack servings    **45 min** active time    **2 hrs 25 min** start to finish

1 cup gluten-free or regular old-fashioned oats (not quick-cooking oats)

½ medium apple, peeled

½ cup apple butter (I use Eden Foods brand.)

4 tablespoons salted butter

¼ cup chia seeds, plus ½ teaspoon for garnish

¼ cup maple syrup

1 tablespoon unsweetened cocoa

1 teaspoon ground cinnamon

½ teaspoon ground turmeric (optional)

¼ teaspoon sea salt, plus more for garnish

3 tablespoons finely chopped candied ginger (optional but awesome)

¼ cup stemmed and finely chopped dried Turkish figs (about 4 figs)

¼ cup finely chopped pitted dried plums (about 6 dried plums)

½ cup roasted pepitas, plus 1 tablespoon, chopped, for garnish

3 tablespoons dark or semisweet chocolate chips

**Prep**  Preheat the oven to 350°F. Lightly oil an 8 × 8-inch square baking pan. Line the baking pan with a square piece of parchment paper, with about 2 inches hanging over each side. Oiling the pan first helps the parchment paper stick. Brush the paper lightly with oil as well.

**Toast the Oats and Prep the Apple**  Line a baking sheet with aluminum foil or parchment paper. Pour the oats onto the baking sheet and spread into an even layer. Bake for 10 minutes, then remove from the oven and place in a medium bowl. Set aside. Keep the oven at 350°F.

While the oats toast, shred the apple with a cheese grater. Place the apple shreds between two layers of paper towels or in a clean tea towel and squeeze out any excess moisture. Remove the apple shreds from the paper towel, place them in a small bowl, and set aside.

**Cook the Apple Base and Make the Bars**  Add the shredded apple, apple butter, butter, chia seeds, maple syrup, cocoa, cinnamon, turmeric (if using), and salt to a medium saucepan. Stir the mixture together over medium-low heat until warm and combined, about 2 to 3 minutes. Remove from the heat and cool for 10 minutes.

Add the oats, candied ginger (if using), figs, and dried plums to the saucepan with the apple mixture, then stir the mixture to combine. Fold in the pepitas until evenly distributed. Using a rubber spatula or wooden spoon, press the mixture firmly into the bottom of the prepared baking pan to form one even layer, about 1 inch thick.

**Bake, Decorate, Cool, and Cut**  Bake the bars for 20 to 25 minutes, until they have firmed up somewhat. They will still feel a bit soft to the touch. Remove the pan from the oven and let cool at room temperature for 30 to 45 minutes.

Once the bars are cooled, melt the chocolate. In a small, microwave-safe ramekin or bowl, heat the chocolate chips in the microwave for 30 seconds, then stir. Continue to microwave in 20-second increments until the chocolate is melted to the point that you can drizzle it from a fork. This should take about 1 minute. Drizzle the chocolate over the bars, then garnish with the chia seeds, chopped pepitas, and lightest sprinkle of sea salt.

Refrigerate the bars in the pan for at least 30 minutes (or freeze for 15 minutes) before cutting the bars into equal-size squares, or triangles if you want a bar that's outside the box.

**Let's Eat!**  Wrap up these homemade bars (or triangles) of bliss the night before the big Apple Cider Century ride and you'll be the coolest kids at the SAG (support and gear) stops. Or make them any time, all the time, because they're the perfect snack for the beach, boat, river, or dunes!

The bars stay chewy-licious when stored for up to 5 days in the refrigerator and are best enjoyed at room temperature. You can also freeze them in an airtight container for up to 1 month.

# Sweets and Treats

Aᴿᴛᴇʀ ᴏɴᴇ sᴜᴍᴍᴇʀ in Harbor Country, I started to wonder if people say "lake life, best life" simply because there are so many occasions to indulge in sweets and treats at the lake!

From snack time after a long day of play to late night s'mores sessions around the fire pit, the next delicious sugar rush is always right around the corner. Now you know why this chapter looks a little longer than the rest!

At Camp Navama there is always a reason to celebrate something with a freshly frosted cake, red rhubarb crisp, chewy, buttery cookies, or the perfect slice of pie.

This collection of recipes is sure to satisfy any sweet tooth, whether you're craving something classic like my 100 Percent Homemade Sugar Pumpkin Pie (page 136) or want to whip up something more whimsical like the Michigan Red Cherry Wine and Goat Cheese Dreamsicles (page 122).

The only thing that makes an already delicious dessert taste even better is picking the fruit yourself. U-pick farms abound in Harbor Country, and I've listed my favorites throughout this chapter. If you want to eat dessert first, that's okay . . . you're at the lake!

# May I Have S'more Please

WE WERE ALL huddled around the fire pit circle at Camp Navama, bodies wrapped in blankets and tummies filled with s'mores. "Okay, everyone put your heads back, take a deep breath, close your eyes, and make a wish on that shooting star!" I said to the friends who were visiting for the weekend from Chicago. Without hesitation, everyone, adults and kiddos, raised their faces skyward, shut their eyes tight, and wished. Normally, those over age 10 might have opted out of the nostalgic ritual, but that's the magic of slowing down in a place like Harbor Country, even for just a few days. It rekindles your spontaneous sense of wonder and awe, one simple pleasure at a time.

Over the summer and well into fall, we hosted many stargazing, s'mores-making sessions. I began to experiment with taking this classic campfire dessert to the next level using a variety of craft chocolate bars and artisanal marshmallows.

I also set out on a mission to make homemade gluten-free s'mores crackers with the taste and texture of the iconic graham. I finally found the key: blending oats into your gluten-free flour gives the crackers that hearty nuttiness you get from graham flour.

So the next time you're planning a s'mores session, in Harbor Country or beyond, slow down, take a breath, and gift yourself the time to make these simple, slightly sweet, craveable crackers.

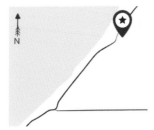

★ Sawyer Home and Garden Center

5865 Sawyer Rd. | Sawyer, MI

★ Infusco Coffee Roasters

5846 Sawyer Rd. | Sawyer, MI

For a great selection of unique chocolate bars and gourmet mallows, head to Sawyer Home and Garden Center in the tiny town of Sawyer. Then, stop by Infusco for an excellent cup of locally roasted coffee.

# Fireside S'mores with Homemade "Graham-Style" Crackers

**4–8** super-s'more servings   **40 min** active time   **1 hr 30 min** start to finish

SPECIAL ITEMS NEEDED

Food processor

Marshmallow skewers for roasting

Fire pit, campfire, bonfire, or fireplace

HOMEMADE "GRAHAM-STYLE" CRACKERS

1¼ cups plus 2 tablespoons gluten-free all-purpose flour *with* xanthan gum or regular all-purpose flour, divided, plus more as needed to form a dough ball (I use Cup4Cup Multipurpose Flour.)

½ cup gluten-free or regular old-fashioned oats

¼ cup light or dark brown sugar

¼ cup granulated sugar

1 teaspoon ground cinnamon

½ teaspoon ground nutmeg

½ teaspoon ground ginger

¼ teaspoon ground allspice

¾ teaspoon baking powder

½ teaspoon baking soda

½ teaspoon salt

6 tablespoons cold salted butter, cut into ⅓-inch cubes

1 tablespoon molasses

1 tablespoon honey

1 teaspoon pure vanilla extract

2 tablespoons almond milk or milk of choice, plus more as needed to form a dough ball

FOR SERVING

2–4 flavors gourmet marshmallows (In a pinch, classic mallows will do.)

2–3 types chocolate bars (Thinner bars melt better.)

TIPS FOR SUCCESS

*A gourmet s'mores kit makes the perfect host gift. Fill mason jars with your favorite mallows and chocolate, add a bag of homemade graham-style crackers, and pat yourself on the back for thinking outside the wine bottle!*

**Prep** Arrange the racks on the top and bottom thirds of the oven and preheat to 325°F. Set two baking sheets aside. Place three sheets of parchment paper, the size of the baking sheets, on a surface nearby to roll out the dough.

**Make the Dough** In a food processor fit with the large chopping blade, add 1¼ cups of the flour and the oats and blend until the mixture is the consistency of flour. Add the brown sugar, granulated sugar, cinnamon, nutmeg, ginger, allspice, baking powder, baking soda, and salt and pulse about 10 times to combine. Scatter the butter cubes over the flour mixture, then blend until the mixture resembles coarse cornmeal. Add the molasses, honey, vanilla, and milk. Blend until the dough comes together to form a ball, scraping down the sides of the bowl as needed with a spatula. *One teaspoon at a time, add more milk or flour as needed until a ball just begins to form.* The dough will be sticky. Use lightly oiled hands to pull the dough from the processor and form a ball.

**Roll Out and Score** Sprinkle the remaining 2 tablespoons of flour on one sheet of parchment paper. Place the dough in the center of the parchment paper and cut the dough in half. Set one piece aside. With floured hands, pat the dough into a rectangular shape, about 1 inch thick. Sprinkle lightly with flour. Place a second piece of parchment paper on top of the dough. With a rolling pin, roll out to an even thickness of ¼ inch. Turn the parchment paper as needed to roll the dough into a rectangular shape. *The dough must be thin or the crackers will be too thick and tough for s'mores.*

Once rolled out, gently pull back the top piece of parchment and use a sharp knife to cut the edges away, leaving a large rectangle with straight, even sides. Use the knife tip to lightly score the dough into squares based on the size of the mallows. *Don't cut all the way through the dough.* Prick each square with a fork in an even pattern. Transfer the parchment paper with the rolled-out crackers to one of the baking sheets. Repeat the process with the remaining dough ball.

*Recipe continues* →

**Bake** Bake the crackers for 15 to 20 minutes, until the edges begin to brown. Halfway through cooking, rotate and swap the two trays to ensure even baking. The centers will still be slightly soft when done. Remove from the oven. Using a sharp chef's knife, immediately cut the crackers into separate squares along the score lines. Cool the crackers completely on the pan before making s'mores. Once cooled, these can be stored in an airtight container at room temperature for 5 days.

**Let's Eat!** On a large tray, arrange a variety of "graham-style" crackers, mallows, and chocolate bars that have been broken into squares to fit the crackers. Gather near the fire and roast mallows using fire-safe skewers. Toast to your liking. Place a square of chocolate on a cracker, top with toasted mallow, and then top with a second cracker. Close your eyes, breathe in the fire, the laughter, and the good times, and take an ooey-gooey bite of bliss.

## Freestyle

These are some of my favorite combinations of marshmallows and chocolate.

Graham + Cinnamon Churro Smashmallow + Dark Chocolate Sea Salt

Graham + Coconut Pineapple Smashmallow + White Chocolate

# No Need to Scream

ONE WEEKEND DURING our first New Buffalo summer, we were hosting friends from L.A. with their kiddos in tow. Meandering the aisles at Barney's Market to stock up for the days ahead, I spotted a variety pack of the classic sugar cereals I grew up on. Immediately it seemed okay to buy them because, obviously, it was for the kids! As it turned out these children preferred cinnamon rolls the size of their heads from Skip's New Buffalo European Farmers Market—and who could blame them? But that left me with eight boxes of uneaten sweet cereal. Yes, I definitely indulged in a bowl or two and yes, it was as good as I remembered.

A few weeks later, inspired by some wildly delicious dairy-free corn almond soft serve I tried in L.A. and an episode of *Chef's Table* highlighting Milk Bar's famous Cereal Milk Soft Serve created by chef and owner Christina Tosi, I decided to make my very own Saturday cereal "nice cream" sprinkled with all the sweet mallow charms Lucky found in his pot of gold at the end of the rainbow.

# Saturday Morning Cereal Nice Cream

**10–12** nostalgic servings　　**1 hr** active time　　**10 hrs** start to finish

Ice cream maker

High-powered blender, like a Vitamix

Fine mesh strainer, at least 6 inches wide

---

3 cups cornflake cereal (preferably natural, such as Erewhon or Nature's Path)

2 teaspoons cornstarch

2½ cups almond milk or milk of choice, divided (For cow milk, use whole or reduced fat.)

2 (13½-ounce) cans full-fat coconut milk

½ cup full-fat coconut cream, thick white cream portion only

¼ cup agave (In a pinch, use granulated sugar or brown sugar.)

1 teaspoon pure vanilla extract

¼ teaspoon sea salt

2 cups Lucky Charms, plus more for topping (Use Golden Grahams or Cinnamon Toast Crunch, if preferred.)

2 tablespoons vodka (Vodka is what helps homemade ice cream stay softer, as it doesn't freeze. If you prefer not to use this ingredient, you can increase vanilla extract to 1 tablespoon. Note that this will slightly change the flavor; nice cream may have an icier texture and will require more time to become "scoopable" at room temperature once frozen.)

TIPS FOR SUCCESS

*This frozen dessert is best enjoyed when freshly churned. If freezing, remove from the freezer about 20 minutes prior to eating.*

**Freeze the Ice Cream Bowl in Advance**  Place the ice cream maker bowl in the freezer at least 12 to 24 hours in advance.

**Prep**  Preheat the oven to 325°F. Line a baking sheet with parchment paper or aluminum foil.

**Toast the Cornflakes**  Spread out the cornflakes in a single layer on the prepared baking sheet. Toast the cornflakes 10 to 12 minutes, until a nutty, toasted scent wafts through your kitchen. Remove from the oven and let cool for 15 minutes.

**Make the Nice Cream Batter**  In a small bowl, whisk together the cornstarch and 2 tablespoons of the almond milk until the mixture is smooth and the cornstarch is dissolved. Set aside.

Add the remaining almond milk, the coconut milk, the coconut cream, the agave, the vanilla extract, and the salt to a medium pot (at least 2 quarts). Bring to a low simmer over medium-high heat, whisking often. Add the cornstarch mixture to the pot and whisk to combine. Bring to a low boil, then continue to cook for about 2 minutes, whisking constantly. Remove from the heat and let cool for 5 minutes, whisking often to prevent a skin from forming on top of the batter. Pour into a large bowl.

**Steep the Cereal**  Add the toasted cornflakes and Lucky Charms to the hot nice cream batter. With a large spoon or rubber spatula, give the cereal a good stir! Let steep for 20 minutes.

**Strain the Milk from the Cereal**  Place a fine mesh strainer over a medium bowl. Working in batches, use a large spoon to scoop the cereal milk mixture into the strainer. Use a rubber spatula to push the majority of the milk through the strainer. The cereal soaks up a lot of the milk, so push firmly, without forcing too much of the softened cereal through the mesh. Discard the cereal mash, rinse the strainer, and continue this process until all the milk is strained. Strain the milk one last time into another medium bowl to remove as much of the cereal grain as possible.

**Chill Out**  Cover the batter and refrigerate for at least 8 hours or overnight. You can also chill the batter in an airtight container or resealable plastic bag. To chill the batter more quickly, make an ice bath by filling a medium bowl half full with ice. Pour the batter into a large resealable plastic bag and close tightly. Set the filled bag on top of the ice. Fill the bowl with cold water until the bag is submerged and refrigerate for at least 4 hours. *The mixture should be 40°F or cooler before churning in the ice cream maker.*

**Make the Nice Cream**  Remove the chilled batter from the refrigerator. Add the vodka and whisk well. Place the chilled ice cream machine bowl into the ice cream maker. Follow the manufacturer's instructions for your machine, choosing the ice cream setting if your machine has different options. Once you've poured the batter into the machine, let the machine churn until the texture is like firm soft serve. This should take 25 to 40 minutes.

**Let's Eat!**  Top with some "Saturday cereal" and enjoy! If freezing, transfer to an airtight container. The nice cream will keep in the freezer for about 3 days. Remove from the freezer 20 minutes prior to eating.

# Rockin' That Rhubarb

I FIRST DISCOVERED rhubarb at age eight while staying with my grandparents one weekend in the little lakeside cottage they called home for the summer. It was growing in the small front yard garden, and I assumed it was red celery until Grandma Willo picked some one morning to make what she called a "rhubarb crisp." While I wasn't crazy about the idea of dessert being made with a vegetable, I didn't express my grave concerns. Shockingly, the tart and tangy rhubarb tasted nothing like celery, and it became a favorite sweet treat with a dollop of creamy vanilla ice cream on top.

The next morning I found my grandma in the kitchen eating a bowl of the crisp. She must have seen the judgmental "dessert for breakfast?" look on my face. "Rhubarb crisp makes a great breakfast," she insisted. "It's made from vegetables!" I was definitely not going to argue with her sage logic.

The first summer we spent in Harbor Country reconnected me with my rhubarb-loving past. As I explored the various farmers markets in early June, I noticed the crimson red stalks were available in abundance, begging to be mixed with sugar and spices and baked into something glorious. Rhubarb crisp quickly became a Camp Navama classic, and every time I make it, I channel Grandma Willo, whose nickname in her younger years was "Red" thanks to her bright rhubarb-colored hair.

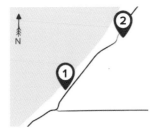

**1 Skip's New Buffalo European Farmers Market**

16710 Lakeshore Rd. | New Buffalo, MI

**2 Sawyer Home and Garden Center**

5865 Sawyer Rd. | Sawyer, MI

I love shopping for local Michigan produce at Skip's New Buffalo European Farmers Market on summer weekends. Another great place to pick up rhubarb in season is Sawyer Home and Garden Center. Note that Michigan's rhubarb season comes and goes quickly, usually beginning in mid-spring and lasting just until early summer.

# Grandma Red's Rhubarb Crisp

🍴 **8–12** delicious servings    🕐 **30 min** active time    ⏳ **1 hr 30 min** start to finish

## RHUBARB FILLING

12–14 stalks fresh rhubarb, ends trimmed and cut into ⅓-inch-thick bite-size slices (7 cups)

½ cup granulated sugar

¼ cup maple syrup

¼ cup orange marmalade (optional but awesome)

2 tablespoons gluten-free all-purpose flour *without* xanthan gum or regular all-purpose flour (I use King Arthur All-Purpose Gluten-Free Flour or Bob's Red Mill Gluten-Free All-Purpose Baking Flour.)

1 tablespoon whiskey, rum, tequila, or pure vanilla extract

½ teaspoon ground cinnamon

½ teaspoon kosher or sea salt

## CRISP TOPPING

¼ cup firmly packed light or dark brown sugar

½ cup gluten-free all-purpose flour *without* xanthan gum or regular all-purpose flour (I use King Arthur All-Purpose Gluten-Free Flour or Bob's Red Mill Gluten-Free All-Purpose Baking Flour.)

1 teaspoon ground cinnamon

1 teaspoon ground ginger

½ teaspoon kosher or sea salt

1⅓ cups gluten-free or regular old-fashioned oats (In a pinch, use quick-cooking oats.)

½ cup (1 stick) cold salted butter, cut into ½-inch cubes

**Prep** Preheat the oven to 375°F. Brush a baking dish lightly with neutral oil such as coconut or grapeseed oil. Set aside.

**Make the Rhubarb Filling** In a large mixing bowl using a wood spoon, toss together the sliced rhubarb, sugar, maple syrup, marmalade (if using), flour, whiskey, cinnamon, and salt until combined and the rhubarb is evenly coated with the flour mixture. Pour into the prepared baking dish and spread into an even layer. Set aside.

**Standing Mixer Method** To make the crisp topping, add the brown sugar, flour, cinnamon, ginger, salt, and oats to the bowl of a standing mixer fit with the paddle attachment. Mix to combine for about 1 minute on medium-low speed. Scatter the butter cubes evenly over the top and continue to mix, moving from low to medium speed, until a coarse, crumbly texture forms and the butter is evenly distributed.

**Manual Method** If making the topping by hand, add the brown sugar, flour, cinnamon, ginger, salt, and oats to a medium mixing bowl and whisk to combine. Scatter the butter cubes evenly over the top and use a pastry cutter or fork and knife to cut in the butter until a coarse, crumbly texture forms and the butter is evenly distributed. This should take 3 to 4 minutes.

**Top and Bake** Distribute the crisp topping in an even layer over the rhubarb filling, ensuring you cover the edges to prevent the rhubarb from bubbling over during baking. Bake for 35 to 40 minutes, until the crisp topping is golden brown. The crisp topping will be soft until it cools. Once done, remove from the oven and cool for at least 30 minutes before serving.

**Let's Eat!** This addictive dessert can be made 1 day ahead. If making ahead of time, store covered in the refrigerator and bring to room temperature before serving. The only thing better than a homemade crisp is one topped with whipped cream or a scoop of your favorite vanilla or maple pecan ice cream. Yumfest!

# U-Pick on a Stick

WHEN ENDLESS BEACH, boat, and bike days arrive followed by warm, delicious nights, baking takes a back seat at Camp Navama, giving way to cooler desserts that don't require the oven. Homemade popsicles really light my fire because of all the creative flavor combinations that can be easily whipped up and frozen into sweet nostalgic treats! And as an unabashed fruit-picking lover, the first time I went cherry picking practically counted as a life event. It was like frolicking through a real-world, way healthier version of Candy Land, and David and I were alllll about it. When we discovered that Michigan is a pretty big deal in the cherry world, we couldn't wait to taste test at every u-pick cherry farm in Harbor Country.

Here are two sweet ways to celebrate Michigan's cherry season and let summer reign!

For more of a party pop, try the Michigan Red Cherry Wine and Goat Cheese Dreamsicles (page 122). It's amazing how well local cherry wine pairs with creamy goat cheese, elevating the creamsicle to dreamsicle status. For kids or the kid in you, give the Cheery Cherry Chocolate Popsicles (page 124) a whirl.

### 1 Nye Heritage Farms and Apple Barn

3151 Niles Rd. | St. Joseph, MI

### 2 St. Julian Winery Tasting Room

9145 Union Pier Rd. | Union Pier, MI

Sweet cherries are typically available in Southwest Michigan and Northwest Indiana from mid-June through July, weather permitting. Among my favorite u-pick farms for sweet cherries is Nye Heritage Farms and Apple Barn. Cherry season comes and goes quickly, so call ahead to make sure the farm still has u-pick sweet cherries available. For the Michigan Red Cherry Wine and Goat Cheese Dreamsicles, pick up a bottle of local Michigan cherry wine at one of the many wineries or tasting rooms in Harbor Country. In Union Pier, I love visiting the St. Julian Winery tasting room. (See more favorite local wineries on the list of my favorite Harbor Country spots on page 225.)

# Michigan Red Cherry Wine and Goat Cheese Dreamsicles

**6–8** dreamy servings    **30 min** active time    **8 hrs 30 min** start to finish

SPECIAL ITEMS NEEDED

Popsicle molds

Popsicle sticks

Blender

GOAT CHEESE MIXTURE

6 ounces crème fraîche

3 ounces goat cheese

⅓ cup almond milk or milk of choice

¼ cup honey or agave

CHERRY MIXTURE

1½ cups fresh pitted cherries or frozen dark sweet pitted cherries, defrosted and juice drained

⅓ cup local Michigan red cherry wine

2 tablespoons honey or agave

TIPS FOR SUCCESS

*Open your mind to a new kind of popsicle! Some people said I was crazy to make a popsicle with goat cheese. Some people swooned and couldn't wait for the recipe. If you like cherries and are a creamsicle fan, give it a go. Your taste buds and foodie friends will thank you.*

**Make the Goat Cheese Mixture**  Place the crème fraîche, goat cheese, almond milk, and honey in a medium saucepan over medium-high heat. Bring to a soft simmer, whisking often, 4 to 5 minutes. Remove from the heat, transfer into a small mixing bowl, and let cool for 15 minutes.

**Make the Cherry Mixture**  Add the cherries, cherry wine, and honey to a blender. Briefly blend on low to medium speed for 20 to 30 seconds. You want some small pieces of cherry remaining to amp up the flavor and texture of your pops! Set aside.

**Make Your Pops**  Fill each popsicle mold about two-thirds full with the goat cheese mixture. Fill the remainder with the cherry mixture. Use a butter knife or the end of a spoon to swirl very lightly, as you still want some separation in the popsicles once they are frozen. Insert the sticks as directed by your popsicle mold set. Freeze for at least 8 hours or overnight.

**Let's Eat!**  Remove from the freezer about 5 to 10 minutes before serving. This makes it easier to release the pops from the molds. Who says you can't have your popsicle and a little wine too?

# Cheery Cherry Chocolate Popsicles

🍴 **6–8** summertime servings   🕐 **30 min** active time   ⧗ **8 hrs 30 min** start to finish

SPECIAL ITEMS NEEDED

Popsicle molds

Popsicle sticks

Blender

3 cups fresh pitted cherries, or 2½ cups frozen dark sweet pitted cherries, defrosted and juice drained

1 cup freshly squeezed orange juice (In a pinch, use store-bought orange juice)

1 tablespoon honey

Pinch sea salt

½ cup semisweet chocolate chips

½ cup white chocolate chips

TIPS FOR SUCCESS

*Lightly oil a tablespoon before measuring the honey. This can be done any time you need to measure a sticky ingredient to ensure the full amount required is added to the recipe.*

**Blend the Popsicle Base**  Add the cherries, orange juice, honey, and salt to the blender. Blend, moving from low to high, until the mixture is smooth and combined, about 2 minutes. There may still be some small pieces of cherry skins, and that's just fine.

**Make Your Pops**  Divide the cherry mixture evenly among the popsicle molds. Insert the sticks as directed by your popsicle mold set. Freeze for at least 8 hours or overnight.

**Melt the Chocolate**  Once your popsicles are frozen, place the semisweet chocolate chips and white chocolate chips into two small microwave-safe bowls. Microwave each bowl for 30 seconds, then stir and continue to microwave in 20-second increments until the chocolate is smooth and you can easily drizzle it from a fork. This should take about 1 to 1½ minutes total. Let cool for 2 to 3 minutes.

**Coat with the Chocolate**  Remove the popsicles from the freezer about 5 minutes before coating with the chocolate. This makes it easier to release the pops from the molds. If a popsicle still seems stuck, you can run it under warm water for 2 to 3 seconds.

Line a baking sheet with parchment paper or aluminum foil. Remove the popsicles from the molds and set on the lined baking sheet. Now it's time to access your inner chocolate artist! Will you dip, drizzle, or paint your pops with the melted chocolates? Work quickly during this step to prevent the pops from melting. A simple fork is the perfect tool for drizzling, or try dipping a popsicle corner in the semisweet chocolate and the opposite corner in the white chocolate.

**Let's Eat!**  Place the baking sheet with the popsicles in the freezer for at least 20 to 30 minutes before serving to harden the chocolate. You can also store the popsicles covered in plastic wrap for up to 1 week!

# Great Crust Is a Must

F OR YEARS, I shied away from making homemade pie crust. Gluten-free or "gluten-full," I had baker's block. But that first summer in Harbor Country, as I carefully washed basket after basket of freshly picked blueberries and raspberries from Garwood Orchards in neighboring Indiana, there was no denying it: pies were begging to be baked! And so mission "conquer the crust" began.

My goal was to make a foolproof recipe for pie crust that could be quickly and easily replicated time and again. The first effort yielded a flavorful but tough crust. David and one of his buddies didn't seem to notice and devoured it anyway.

Onward. Five trials and several weekends later, I pulled a freshly baked pie from the oven made with late summer Ginger Gold apples from Springhope Farm. After taking one bite, I recognized the unmistakable taste of tender, flaky success! Gluten-free or gluten-full, this crust is an all-butter beauty that can be made using a standing mixer or by hand.

# Easy as Pie Crust

🍴 **1** flaky, buttery pie crust    🕐 **40 min** active time    ⏳ **1 hr** start to finish

Standing mixer

1⅛ cups (1 stick plus 2 tablespoons) very cold salted butter, cut into ⅓-inch cubes

1⅓ cups gluten-free all-purpose flour *with* xanthan gum or regular all-purpose flour, plus more as needed (I use Cup4Cup Multipurpose Flour or Bob's Red Mill 1 to 1 Baking Flour.)

2 tablespoons granulated sugar

¼ teaspoon kosher or sea salt

2–3 tablespoons ice water (ice removed)

**TIPS FOR SUCCESS**

*Make sure your butter is very cold.*

*If you're baking solo, fold the parchment paper edge over the end of the table or counter and press your waist against it to hold the paper still while you roll it out. To roll out a pie crust evenly, apply even pressure across the rolling pin as you roll forward and back again, turning the disk of dough as needed.*

**Standing Mixer Method**   Place the cold, cubed butter in the freezer for 10 minutes. Add the flour, sugar, and salt to the bowl of a standing mixer fit with the paddle attachment. Mix on medium speed for 1 minute, until evenly blended. Pause the mixer and scatter the cold butter cubes evenly across the flour. Gently toss with a spoon to coat the butter pieces in flour. Mix on medium-low speed for about 3 minutes, or until the flour-butter mixture resembles coarse sand and the butter pieces are the size of green peas. Use a fork or pastry cutter to break up any remaining butter pieces that look too large. With the mixer on low, slowly drizzle in the ice water, 1 tablespoon at a time, and mix on low to medium-low speed until the dough just pulls together, barely forming a ball. Don't overmix or the crust will be tough.

**Create a Work Surface to Roll Out the Crust**   Place two pieces of parchment paper, each piece about 20 inches long, side by side on a flat surface. Sprinkle one sheet lightly with your flour of choice. Set a rolling pin nearby.

**Rest the Dough**   Transfer the dough ball to the floured parchment paper and form into a ball. Pat the ball into a flattened disk about ¾ inch thick. Wrap the dough in plastic wrap and refrigerate for 20 minutes. (At this stage, the dough can be refrigerated for several hours or overnight if desired, but remove from the refrigerator about 30 minutes before rolling out.)

**Roll Out the Dough**   Remove the dough from the refrigerator. Sprinkle a bit more flour on the parchment paper and place the disk in the center of the parchment paper. Sprinkle the top of the disk and rolling pin lightly with flour as needed (not too much or the dough will be tough), then cover the disk with the second sheet of parchment paper. Roll out into a circle about 12 inches wide and ⅓ inch thick, turning the disk as needed. Once you've rolled it out, hold a pie pan over the center of the dough to ensure it's large enough to cover the pan.

**Rolling Pin Transfer Trick**   Use your rolling pin to transfer the dough to the pie pan by placing the rolling pin at one end of the dough disk. Pull up the parchment paper at that end to help the dough roll up and over the pin, and continue to turn the rolling pin with the other hand until most of your dough is around the pin. Use both hands to gently drape the dough over the pie pan, allowing it to settle into the center and edges. Softly press the dough into the pan, smoothing out any bubbles. Trim the edges as needed with a sharp knife. Use your fingers to crimp the edges into a wavy, fluted design (see photo on page 127), or press the edges down and lightly imprint them with a fork. If the dough doesn't easily pull away from the parchment paper as you try to transfer it to the pie pan, refrigerate the rolled-out dough sheet for another 10 minutes before placing it in the pie pan.

## Freestyle

### Double Pie Crust Version

Double the recipe and cut the dough ball in half. Follow the "Roll Out the Dough" directions. Line a pie pan with 1 crust. Pat the second ball into a disk and refrigerate until ready to use. Remove from the refrigerator 30 minutes prior to use.

### By-Hand Method

If you don't have a standing mixer, make this crust by hand.

Place the cold, cubed butter in the freezer for 10 minutes. In a large bowl, whisk together the flour, sugar, and salt. Scatter the cold butter cubes evenly across the flour mixture. Use a pastry cutter or two knives to cut the butter into the flour mixture until the texture resembles coarse sand and the butter pieces are no larger than green peas. (Avoid using hands, as they make butter too warm.) Drizzle in the ice water, 1 tablespoon at a time, and mix with a fork or pastry cutter until the dough just pulls together, barely forming a ball. Don't overmix or the crust will be tough.

Follow the rest of the directions, starting with the step "Create a Work Surface to Roll Out the Crust."

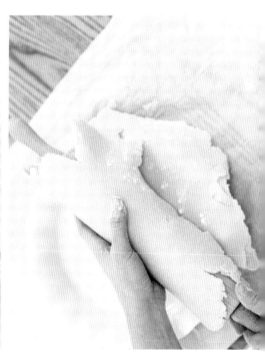

# You're the Apple of My Pie

L ET ME TELL you a secret. While we hosted a ton of friends and family during our first New Buffalo summer, I was extra excited to spend several days with three-year-old Bella, the daughter of the Olsons, our good friends in Chicago.

Before Bella visited Camp Navama for the weekend, this was *my* apple pie. I'd spent weeks perfecting the Easy as Pie Crust recipe (page 128) and creating my dream pie with freshly picked apples, extra ginger, and our favorite locally made maple syrup from **Journeyman Distillery** in Three Oaks.

Word on the street was that this toddler with a sweet tooth was ready to bake an apple pie. I was definitely up for the challenge! Labor Day weekend arrived and we whisked the Olson family off to **Twin Maple Orchards** in Galien, Michigan, where Bella picked and ate her weight in apples.

Back at the house, my little sous chef perched on the kitchen counter. We peeled the apples, chilled the butter, rolled the dough, and baked the ultimate apple pie, which I knew right then and there would always be Bella's Maple Apple Pie.

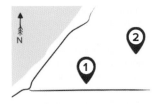

**1 Journeyman Distillery and Staymaker Restaurant**

109 Generations Dr. | Three Oaks, MI

**2 Twin Maple Orchards**

15352 Cleveland Ave. | Galien, MI

I truly believe a recipe is only as good as the ingredients it contains, and since discovering Journeyman Distillery's exceptional maple syrup, it's been hard to use anything else. Aged in bourbon barrels, this 100 percent pure maple syrup is now a permanent part of my pantry. You can pick up a bottle at Staymaker, the distillery's restaurant. Twin Maple Orchards, where I picked the apples for this recipe, has been owned by the Zielbauer family for over 40 years. Just a short drive from Harbor Country, families come for some of the best u-pick apples and plums around and for the produce on sale at the Zielbauers' farmstand. Bring the kids for a fun tractor ride into the orchards. Come July, Twin Maple also has some of the sweetest heirloom tomatoes in Michigan.

# Bella's Maple Apple Pie

🍴 **6–8** apple-icious servings   🕐 **1 hr** active time   ⏳ **3 hrs** start to finish

SPECIAL ITEMS NEEDED

Apple peeler

Pie crust shield

## PIE CRUST

2 recipes Easy as Pie Crust (page 128) , made with 2 teaspoons ground cinnamon added to the flour mixture, or your favorite store-bought pie crust

## APPLE FILLING

6 medium apples (Use a blend of tart apples such as Honeycrisp, Melrose, Jonagold, Ginger Gold, Cortland, Winesap, or Granny Smith.)

¼ cup firmly packed dark brown sugar (In a pinch, use light brown sugar.)

¼ cup maple syrup

2 tablespoons freshly squeezed lemon juice

2 teaspoons balsamic vinegar

2 tablespoons cornstarch, all-purpose gluten-free flour, or regular all-purpose flour

2 teaspoons ground cinnamon

2 teaspoons ground ginger

½ teaspoon kosher salt

## EGG WASH

1 egg white

2 tablespoons water

## CINNAMON SUGAR TOPPING

2 tablespoons granulated sugar

2 teaspoons ground cinnamon

### TIPS FOR SUCCESS

*Find a toddler who's serious about apple pie to be your sous chef.*

*Harbor Country's apple orchards make owning an apple peeler 100 percent worth it. The $10 to $20 investment will save you time, and your fingers will thank you. Locally, pick up a simple manual hand-crank peeler at Sawyer Home and Garden Center in the fall. Peeling attachments for a standing mixer also work well.*

**Conquer the Crust** Line an 8- or 9-inch pie pan with 1 circle of pie dough. Set aside.

**Prep the Apples** Peel, core, and slice the apples into wedges about 1 inch wide. After peeling, I love using an apple slicer that both slices and cores the apples. Cut each wedge crosswise into ⅓-inch-thick slices, or use a food processor, fit with the slicing blade, to cut the apples into bite-size pieces.

**Make the Apple Filling** Place the apples in a large mixing bowl. Add the brown sugar, maple syrup, lemon juice, balsamic vinegar, cornstarch, cinnamon, ginger, and salt. Use a wooden spoon or spatula to combine, ensuring the apples are evenly coated. Loosely cover with a paper towel or clean dish towel. Let stand for 30 minutes at room temperature. Drain the juice from the apples before filling the pie crust.

**Preheat the Oven** Arrange the oven rack in the lower third of oven, one position higher than the bottom. Preheat the oven to 400°F.

**Make the Pie** Spoon the drained apples into the pie crust, mounding them slightly in the center and filling to about ½ inch below the brim of the pie pan. Top with the second pie dough circle and use your fingers to crimp the edges together in a scalloped pattern, ensuring the crust seams are pressed tight so nothing leaks out during baking. Use a sharp knife to make 4 vertical 1-inch slits, about 2 inches apart, in the center of the pie.

**Make the Egg Wash and Cinnamon Sugar Topping** In a small bowl, use a fork to whisk together the egg white and water until foamy. Brush the pie crust with a thin layer of the egg wash using a basting brush, then mix the granulated sugar with the cinnamon and sprinkle evenly over the pie.

**Bake That Pie!** Use a pie crust shield or four strips of aluminum foil (12 inches long and 2 inches wide) to cover the edges of the crust to prevent burning. Bake the pie for 45 minutes, then remove the shields and bake for another 10 to 15 minutes, until the crust is lightly golden brown.

**Let's Eat!** Let the pie cool for at least 1 hour before serving. If you really wanna show love through dessert, consider serving this pie with whipped cream, ice cream, or both!

# Very Pie Expectations

"WHAT'S A SUGAR PUMPKIN?!" David asked, staring at piles and piles of bright orange globes the size of cantaloupes at Dinges' Fall Harvest, Harbor Country's iconic pumpkin patch.

"Those are pie pumpkins," I told him. He looked confused. "You know the canned stuff comes from real pumpkins, right?"

"Yeah, I just . . . can you make us pie with these tonight?" he asked with a hungry, hopeful grin.

Between you and me, I'd never made pie using fresh pumpkin, but I wasn't about to spill those beans! "Sure, yeah, yum!" I picked out four perfect little sugar pumpkins, and while David tracked down farmer Lee Dinges to see if we could indeed buy his last white turkey for Thanksgiving, I went to pay.

That's when I met Elaine Dinges, wife of Lee. Something told me the queen of this pumpkin patch would have a few hints about baking a from-scratch pumpkin pie. She happily handed me a printed recipe, and with my cheat sheet in hand, I headed into the kitchen confidently, ready to conquer my first 100 Percent Homemade Sugar Pumpkin Pie. It can also be made gluten- and dairy-free, making this the perfect recipe for all pumpkin pie lovers. Now step right up and take the 100 percent homemade pumpkin pie challenge!

# 100 Percent Homemade Sugar Pumpkin Pie

🍴 **6–8** scrumptious servings   🕐 **1 hr 30 min** active time   ⧖ **5 hr** start to finish

## SPECIAL ITEMS NEEDED

High-powered blender or food processor (necessary if using fresh pumpkin)

Pie weight or dry beans

---

1 (2–3 pound) sugar pumpkin (In a pinch, use 3 cups unsweetened canned pumpkin purée.)

1 recipe Easy as Pie Crust (page 128)

¼ cup coconut sugar or light or dark brown sugar

¼ cup maple syrup

¼ cup full-fat coconut milk or whole milk

2 eggs

1 egg yolk

1 tablespoon pumpkin pie spice

1 teaspoon ground cinnamon

½ teaspoon kosher or sea salt

¼ teaspoon ground cloves (optional)

**Prep** Preheat the oven to 375°F and line a baking sheet with aluminum foil or parchment paper. Brush it with oil. Set aside.

**Roast the Pumpkin** Cut a small circle around the top of the pumpkin and remove the stem. Slice the pumpkin in half, from top to bottom, and scoop out all the seeds. Place the two halves cut side down on the baking sheet and bake for 40 to 50 minutes, until the pumpkin is fork tender. Cool until just warm, about 20 to 30 minutes. Raise the oven temperature to 425°F once the pumpkin is done baking.

**Prep the Pie Crust and Blind Bake** Line an 8- or 9-inch pie pan with the circle of pie dough. Dock the dough by pricking the bottom and sides evenly with a fork to release steam during blind baking. To blind bake, line the entire crust with a sheet of parchment paper (use aluminum foil in a pinch), fill with pie weights or dried beans (this prevents the crust bottom from bubbling), and bake at 425°F for 15 minutes. Let cool for 5 to 10 minutes, then gently remove the weights and parchment paper. Reduce the oven temperature to 350°F.

**Make the Pie Filling** While the crust blind bakes, make your pie filling! Use a large metal spoon or ice cream scoop to scrape all the pumpkin from the skin into a high-powered blender or food processor. Blend on medium-high until puréed and creamy-smooth. If using a regular blender, work in small batches. Remove the puréed pumpkin from the blender, place in a bowl, and set aside.

Rinse the blender or food processor to clean it, then add 3 cups of the fresh pumpkin purée, the sugar, the maple syrup, the coconut milk, the eggs and yolk, the pumpkin pie spice, the cinnamon, the salt, and the cloves (if using). Blend or process on medium-high until smooth, scraping down the sides as needed.

**Bake That Pie!** Pour the filling into the blind-baked crust, cover the edges loosely with aluminum foil strips or a pie crust shield to prevent burning, and bake at 350°F for about 1 hour, or until a toothpick inserted between the center and the edge of the pie comes out clean. *Special Note: When the pie is ready to be removed from the oven, the filling will still jiggle slightly in the center. (The center is 2 to 3 inches in diameter.)* The pie will continue to cook and fully set once you remove it from the oven, so resist the temptation to overbake your delicious dessert!

**Cool** Let the pie cool for at least 2 hours so it fully sets before serving.

**Let's Eat!** Elevate this pumpkin pie to rock star status by serving it with your favorite ice cream! I love the dairy-free, dreamy, creamy Mmm . . . Maple Pecan by NadaMoo. Store the pie covered in the refrigerator for 3 to 4 days.

# A Cookie Walks into a Bar . . .

WHEN I STARTED Cookies Couture at the ripe age of 22, the idea was to let my customers concoct their dream cookie, something that really spoke to their inner cookie monsters. This recipe was originally developed for a musician from the South who wanted a thick, chewy, buttery oatmeal raisin cookie that honored his southern roots. I decided to soak the raisins in Southern Comfort whiskey, which made this baked good a little bit boozy and super soft.

In the dead of our first winter in New Buffalo, baking was something I turned to often to warm up our hearts and our home! While writing this book, I revisited many of the recipes from my cookie company days and decided to give this one a whirl.

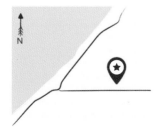

### ★ Journeyman Distillery

109 Generations Dr. | Three Oaks, MI

I use Journeyman Featherbone Bourbon Whiskey, made at Journeyman Distillery in Three Oaks, in this recipe. Sure, you can use any old whiskey you'd like, but if you want to bake in the spirit of Harbor Country, then you must use a Harbor Country spirit.

# Brown Sugar Oatmeal Cookies with Whiskey Raisins

🍴 **24** boozy servings    🕐 **45 min** active time    ⏳ **3 hrs** start to finish

SPECIAL ITEMS NEEDED

Large #20 ice cream scoop

WHISKEY RAISINS

1½ cups raisins (I use Thompson Seedless Raisins.)

1¼ cups whiskey of choice (I use local Journeyman Featherbone Bourbon Whiskey.)

BROWN SUGAR OATMEAL COOKIES

1½ cups plus 2 tablespoons gluten-free all-purpose flour *with* xanthan gum or regular all-purpose flour (I use Cup4Cup Multipurpose Flour.)

½ teaspoon baking soda

½ teaspoon baking powder

1 teaspoon ground cinnamon

1 teaspoon pumpkin pie spice

½ teaspoon kosher salt (In a pinch, any salt will do.)

1 cup (2 sticks) salted butter, softened in the microwave for about 20 seconds

1 cup firmly packed light brown sugar (In a pinch, use dark brown sugar.)

¼ cup granulated sugar

2 eggs

3 cups gluten-free or regular old-fashioned oats

TIPS FOR SUCCESS

*For a tender cookie, avoid overmixing your dough. This means beating the butter and sugar until just creamed, the eggs until just incorporated, and the flour until just combined and the dough looks uniform. Also, chilling this dough makes all the difference to get thick, chewy cookies.*

**Cook and Soak the Whiskey Raisins** Place the raisins in a small pot with the whiskey. Stir, then bring to a strong simmer over medium-high heat. Reduce the heat to low, cover, and simmer for 15 minutes. Remove from the heat and let the raisins soak for 2 hours. Drain the raisins well (reserving the whiskey for a cookie-inspired cocktail if you like). Press the raisins gently with a paper towel or clean kitchen towel to soak up any excess whiskey. *Special Note: This step is important, as too much alcohol can cause the cookie to crumble, literally.*

**Prep** Arrange the racks on the top and bottom thirds of the oven. Preheat the oven to 350°F. Line two baking sheets with parchment paper or aluminum foil. Set aside.

**Make the Dough and Chill Out** In a medium bowl, whisk together the flour, baking soda, baking powder, cinnamon, pumpkin pie spice, and salt. Set aside.

In the bowl of a standing mixer fit with the paddle attachment on medium speed (or in a medium bowl using an electric hand mixer or whisk), cream together the butter, brown sugar, and granulated sugar until combined, 2 to 3 minutes, scraping down the sides as needed. Add the eggs and beat on low to medium speed until just combined. Add the flour mixture to the butter mixture and beat, moving from low to medium-high speed, until just combined. Add the oats and beat on medium speed until combined, about 1 minute. Add the whiskey raisins to the bowl and use a spatula or wooden spoon to manually fold in the raisins until evenly distributed throughout the dough.

Place the bowl in the refrigerator for 30 minutes before scooping the dough.

**Bake** Drop scoops of the dough, about ¼ cup each, onto the prepared baking sheets using an oiled measuring cup, ice cream scoop, or large spoon. The dough balls should be about 2 inches apart. Each sheet will hold about 9 cookies. Bake for about 13 to 15 minutes total, until the edges are slightly golden and lift up easily with a spatula. *Halfway through baking, rotate the trays and swap positions to ensure even cooking.* When done, the cookies will still be quite soft in the center, but they will set as they cool.

**Cool** Remove from the oven and let cool for at least 15 minutes before eating. Yes, this might feel like the longest 15 minutes of your life, but with patience comes delicious rewards!

**Let's Eat!** Enjoy these cookies on the porch with a chilled glass of almond milk or dairy milk—or Journeyman Featherbone Bourbon Whiskey on the rocks if you're adulting! Whatever feels right in the moment, do that.

# These Apples Are
# Lovin' the Oven

O UR GREAT FRIEND Mike Misrachi was in town visiting from Los Angeles and my hopeful husband wanted me to bake them a treat . . . at 10:30 p.m. I stood in my kitchen surrounded by bags and bags of u-pick apples that guests visiting us at the lake definitely wanted to pick but "just couldn't take on the plane." What could I make with apples and minimal effort that the boys would consider a treat? And then, with one flashback to my seven-year-old self, I knew.

Baked apples are like a secret dessert. Growing up, when something like ice cream or cookies wasn't open for discussion, I could usually get my mom to whip up a baked apple if I really wanted something sweet. Excited to recreate my mom's magical recipe with freshly picked fruit, I set about coring the apples, softening some butter, and whisking together a spiced brown sugar filling with oats and pecans. Soon the apples were baking away and I was relaxing with a mug of hot tea, waiting for the scent of caramelized goodness to tell us our treat was ready to eat!

**1 Lehman's Orchard**

2280 Portage Rd. | Niles, MI

**2 Lemon Creek Winery and Farm Market**

533 E. Lemon Creek Rd. | Berrien Springs, MI

For some of the best u-pick apple adventures in Harbor Country, visit Lehman's Orchard. I also love Lemon Creek Winery and Farm Market, where you can pick up a bottle of local Michigan wine along with your produce. Bring home their cherry wine to make my Michigan Red Cherry Wine and Goat Cheese Dreamsicles (page 122).

# Autumn Baked Apples with Caramelized Pecan Oat Crumble

¶¶ **6** heart-warming servings    ⏱ **30 min** active time    ⧗ **1 hr 30 min** start to finish

SPECIAL ITEMS NEEDED

Apple corer or melon baller

10- to 12-inch cast iron skillet, or 2 (6-inch) cast iron skillets

---

½ cup plus 2 tablespoons gluten-free or regular old-fashioned oats (In a pinch, use quick-cooking oats.)

½ cup firmly packed light or dark brown sugar

½ cup chopped pecans

2 teaspoons ground cinnamon

½ teaspoon kosher salt

¼ teaspoon ground cloves (optional)

4 medium apples (Use softer, sweeter apples such as Golden Delicious, Honeycrisp, or Ginger Gold)

4 tablespoons cold salted butter

½ cup apple cider (In a pinch, use apple juice or water.)

## Freestyle

Add ⅓ cup finely chopped candied ginger to the brown sugar mixture.

Drop 1 tablespoon of your favorite nut butter at the bottom of each apple before stuffing with the brown sugar mixture.

Add ⅓ cup chopped dried cherries or dried cranberries to the brown sugar mixture.

TIPS FOR SUCCESS

*Resist cooking the apples too long or they will burst open!*

**Prep** Place a 10- to 12-inch cast iron skillet in the oven on the middle rack, then preheat the oven to 375°F. You can also use an 8 × 8-inch oven-safe baking dish brushed with oil, but there is no need to place this in the oven prior to baking the apples.

**Make the Oat Filling** Add the oats, brown sugar, pecans, cinnamon, salt, and cloves (if using) to a medium mixing bowl. Stir well to combine. Set aside.

**Core the Apples to Hold the Stuffing** Use a melon baller (my preference), apple corer, or sharp paring knife to remove the cores from the apples without piercing holes through the bottom. This part takes patience, so I remind myself, "Go slow and enjoy the process, Lindsay, so your apples don't leak!" Scoop out enough flesh from each apple to hold about ⅓ cup of the crumble. If the apple doesn't easily stand up, slice a little off the bottom to make it flat. If you accidently *do* poke a hole all the way through, "patch" the hole with a dried fig, dried plum, or small scoop of nut butter.

**Stuff the Apples** Cut the cold butter into 8 equal slices, ½ tablespoon each. Use a spoon to fill each apple halfway full with the brown sugar mixture. Put 1 slice of the butter in each apple, then fill the apples with the remaining stuffing. Place the remaining slices of butter on top of each apple.

**Bake the Apples Covered** Remove the cast iron skillet from the oven using heavy-duty oven mitts. Please be very careful! This skillet is SUPER HOT. Leave the mitts over the handle to prevent grabbing it by accident! Pour the apple cider into the bottom of the skillet or pan. Place the apples in the cast iron skillet or oven-safe baking dish. The apples should stand up and be evenly spaced. Put on oven mitts to cover the apples with aluminum foil. Bake for 25 minutes.

**Bake the Apples Uncovered** Carefully remove the foil and bake the apples uncovered for another 20 minutes, or until a knife easily pierces the apples and the fruit is tender but not mushy. When done, the skin will be somewhat wrinkled. Let cool for about 15 minutes before serving.

**Let's Eat!** Serve the baked apples in bowls with a knife and fork. Top with a dollop of whipped cream or a scoop of your favorite ice cream. For kiddos and easy eating in general, slice the baked apples into bite-size pieces in a bowl before adding whipped or ice cream and serving. Yum, yum, yum. If not immediately serving, these can be made 1 day ahead and stored covered in the refrigerator, then reheated in the microwave for 3 to 4 minutes or in a 350°F oven until warm.

# Cake by the Lake

FOR ME, nothing screams CELEBRATION like a heavily frosted, rainbow-sprinkle-covered, sugar-buzz-guaranteed cake! I've always wondered why this whimsical cake is typically restricted to birthdays. Why on this good earth would anyone want to limit how often they enjoyed such a fantastic baked good to a few times a year? Ammiiright?!

David and I found more reasons to celebrate in 12 months in Harbor Country than we had living in Chicago for three years! There's something about the energy that meanders down Red Arrow Highway, ebbs and flows with the waves on the shoreline, and darts through the forest with the squirrels and fireflies that inspires you to celebrate more moments.

We celebrated big things, like our first wedding anniversary, medium things, like hosting guests from out of town and concerts at **The Acorn Theater** in Three Oaks, Michigan, and small things, like relishing a hot mug of coffee lakeside in the early morning sunshine. Our home in New Buffalo reminded us how much there is to celebrate daily, and for that we're forever grateful to Harbor Country and the splendid community that exists here.

With that, it's my pleasure to introduce this super simple recipe that makes it easier than ever to celebrate every day like it's your birthday!

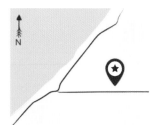

## ★ The Acorn Theater

107 Generation Dr. | Three Oaks, MI

If you've never experienced The Acorn Theater, book a show soon. This magical creative space continually provides Harbor Country with excellent entertainment like memorable music groups, open mic nights, comedy shows, and dramas. The main auditorium seats about 100 people, and some awesome acts, as well as up-and-coming local stars, perform here before heading to Chicago.

# Every Day's My Birthday Cake

🍴 **10–12** celebratory servings    🕐 **1 hr** active time    ⏳ **2 hrs** start to finish

---

SPECIAL ITEMS NEEDED

2 (8- or 9-inch) cast iron skillets
or round cake pans, or
1 (9 × 13 × 2-inch) cake pan

---

CAKE

1–2 boxes favorite yellow cake
mix (depending on size of
mix and desired quantity.)

1 teaspoon pure vanilla extract

½ teaspoon almond extract

⅓ cup colorful sprinkles,
plus more for frosting

RICH CHOCOLATE FROSTING

⅓ cup semisweet chocolate chips

6½ cups confectioners' sugar,
sifted, plus more as needed

1 cup (2 sticks) salted butter,
softened in the microwave
for about 20 seconds

¼ cup plus 1 tablespoon boiling
water, plus more as needed to
reach desired consistency

1 tablespoon pure vanilla extract

⅛ teaspoon kosher or sea
salt, plus more to taste

½ cup unsweetened cocoa powder

VERY VANILLA FROSTING

6½ cups confectioners' sugar,
sifted, plus more as needed

1 cup (2 sticks) salted butter,
softened in the microwave
for about 20 seconds

¼ cup boiling water, plus
more as needed to reach
desired consistency

1 tablespoon pure vanilla extract

¼ teaspoon kosher or sea salt

TIPS FOR SUCCESS

*I include two frosting recipes here, so you can make either Rich Chocolate Frosting or Very Vanilla Frosting, whichever you prefer! The Freestyle box also provides directions if you want to make half vanilla and half chocolate frosting.*

*Using a cake mix is the secret to having your cake and hammock time, too. I add vanilla and almond extract to amp up the flavor. The fabulous from-scratch frosting pairs perfectly with the cake, but don't be afraid to frost brownies, cookies, or s'mores, too! You might just want a shot of frosting . . . and that's okay. No judgment here, friends!*

*In the summer I love grilling these cakes in cast iron skillets to keep my kitchen cool. It's also a fun way to serve the cake. You can bake the cake in cast iron in the oven, if preferred. Alternatively, use regular cake pans in the oven.*

*This frosting recipe will frost 2 (8- or 9-inch) single-layer cakes, 1 (8- or 9-inch) double-layer cake, or 1 (9 × 13 × 2-inch) cake. You will also have some extra frosting for piping or for a later use.*

*No sifter? No problem! In the bowl of a standing mixer fit with the whisk attachment, whisk the confectioners' sugar for 2 to 3 minutes to fluff it up a bit.*

**Prep the Cast Iron Skillets or Cake Pans** If using cast iron skillets, place them on the center of a grill or in the oven on the middle rack. (If using cake pans, do not place in the grill or oven while preheating.) Preheat the grill or oven according to the temperature listed on the cake mix package.

**Make the Cake** Make the cake batter according to the package directions, adding the vanilla and almond extract when you add the eggs or liquid called for on the package. Once the batter is made, fold in the sprinkles gently to evenly distribute them. Don't overstir or the colors will bleed. Divide the batter evenly between the two preheated cast iron skillets (using heavy-duty oven mitts as the skillets are HOT!) or the two round cake pans.

**On the Grill** Bake the cast iron skillets about 30 to 40 minutes, until a toothpick inserted into the center comes out clean.

**In the Oven** Bake according to the time on the package, or until a toothpick inserted into the center comes out clean.

Once done, remove from the grill or oven and let cool.

*Recipe continues*

**Make the Rich Chocolate Frosting**  If making the chocolate frosting, in a small, microwave-safe ramekin or bowl, heat the chocolate chips for 30 seconds, then stir. Continue to microwave in 30-second increments until the chocolate is melted and smooth, about 1 to 2 minutes. Set aside.

In a medium bowl using an electric handheld mixer or a standing mixer fit with the paddle attachment, mix the confectioners' sugar, softened butter, boiling water, vanilla, and salt on low until combined. Raise the speed to medium and whip for 4 to 5 minutes, until creamy, scraping the sides as needed. *Avoid mixing at high speed or the frosting develops too many air bubbles.* Taste test! Add additional salt to taste and more boiling water as needed, 1 tablespoon at a time, to create desired consistency. Too thin? Whip in more confectioners' sugar, 1 tablespoon at a time.

Add the cocoa to the frosting in the mixing bowl and beat, moving from low to medium speed, until just combined. Pause the mixer, add the melted chocolate to the bowl, and mix on medium speed until smooth and combined, about 2 to 3 minutes. Scrape down the sides of the bowl as needed and use a spatula to ensure all the frosting from the bottom of the bowl is combined with the chocolate.

If not frosting the cake within 1 hour, cover the frosting tightly and refrigerate.

**Make the Very Vanilla Frosting**  If making the vanilla frosting, in a medium bowl using an electric handheld mixer or a standing mixer fit with the paddle attachment, mix the confectioners' sugar, softened butter, boiling water, vanilla, and salt on low until combined. Raise the speed to medium and whip for 4 to 5 minutes, until creamy, scraping the sides as needed. *Avoid mixing at high speed or the frosting develops too many air bubbles.* Taste test! Add additional salt to taste and more boiling water as needed, 1 tablespoon at a time, to create desired consistency. Too thin? Whip in more confectioners' sugar, 1 tablespoon at a time.

If not frosting the cake within 1 hour, cover the frosting tightly and refrigerate.

**Let's Eat!**  Frost your cooled cakes evenly using a frosting spatula or butter knife. Feeling fancy? Whip out a piping bag fit with the large star tip and show off those cake art skills. Decorate with sprinkles before the frosting dries! The frosting can be refrigerated in an airtight container for up to 5 days. Bring to room temperature and whip again on medium speed before using.

# Raise a Glass

THERE ARE SO MANY moments to savor in Harbor Country—a sunrise run on the beach, morning coffee with friends on the screened porch, and of course cocktail (or mocktail!) hour spent watching the sky paint itself orange and green as the sun sinks below the horizon.

The drinks in this chapter keep you hydrated by day and let the good times roll well into the night. And my mocktail recipes made with Fruitbelt, a unique sparkling tonic created with Michigan apples, cherries, and special "orchard bitters," are perfect for everyone, including the kids!

The next time you raise a glass, wherever your Harbor Country may be, savor the moment and make a toast to life's simple joys, like sipping hot coffee through a sweet layer of melted marshmallow, curled up on the couch, anticipating the unplanned day of relaxation and play ahead.

At Camp Navama, I love introducing our houseguests to new things, whether it's paddleboarding for the first time or a large glass of hyper-hydrating lemon elixir before their morning cup of java! Lemon juice helps to balance pH levels in the body and is a rich source of potassium and vitamin C.

After about one week of skeptically drinking a cup each morning, David became a believer and now craves this liquid gold daily. Feel free to alternate with the Spiced Apple Cider Elixir (page 156) and remember that hydrated people are happy people!

# Magic Morning Lemon Elixir

🥛 **2** invigorating servings    ⏳ **10 min** start to finish

3 cups water

Juice of 1 lemon

1–2 tablespoons honey or maple syrup, plus more to taste

1 teaspoon ground turmeric (known to be anti-inflammatory)

Pinch ground cayenne pepper (optional for heat seekers)

Ice, if serving cold

Strips of lemon peel, for garnish

**Cold Elixir**  In a small pitcher, whisk together the water, lemon juice, honey, turmeric, and cayenne (if using) until the honey is dissolved. Pour into two glasses over the ice and serve with your most fun straws. Find a warm spot in the sun to sit, sip, and treat yourself to this healthy indulgence. This drink can also be enjoyed at room temperature.

**Hot Elixir**  In a small pot over medium heat, whisk together the water, lemon juice, honey, turmeric, and cayenne (if using) and heat for 3 to 5 minutes, until just steaming. Remove from the heat and pour into two of your favorite mugs. Find a cozy corner to enjoy while taking a moment for yourself and your health before you begin the day.

MOVE OVER, COFFEE (at least until I have my elixir). There's a new morning pick-me-up in town. It's all kinds of healthy and delicious, too, once you acquire a taste for tang. If you're a kombucha lover, this drink will immediately make you smile. If not, give it a few days and I promise you'll quickly cross over to the apple cider side. Apple cider vinegar has long been touted as having a variety of health benefits, but since we're at the lake I'll keep things light. Let's just say that an apple cider elixir a day keeps low energy away, so we have plenty of time to party and play!

## Spiced Apple Cider Elixir

**2** soul-soothing servings    ⧖ **10 min** start to finish

3 cups water

2 tablespoons apple cider vinegar (I love Bragg brand. Use more or less to taste.)

1 tablespoon maple syrup

½ teaspoon ground ginger

½ teaspoon ground cinnamon

Pinch ground cayenne pepper (optional, for heat seekers)

2 thin slices of apple, cut in circles (Any apple variety will do.)

**Hot Elixir** In a small pot over medium heat, whisk together the water, apple cider vinegar, maple syrup, ginger, cinnamon, and cayenne (if using) and heat for 3 to 5 minutes, until just steaming. Remove from the heat, pour into two of your favorite mugs, and top with a slice of apple.

**Cool Elixir** In a small pitcher, whisk together the water, apple cider vinegar, maple syrup, ginger, cinnamon, and cayenne (if using). Pour into two glasses and top with a slice of apple. The elixir should be enjoyed at room temperature for maximum health benefits, but can also be sipped over ice.

T HE CAFÉ AU LAIT, composed of half drip coffee, half steamed milk, has been my go-to blood of the bean beverage since college. Over the years, I've continued to test, tweak, and modify my recipe for the perfect café au lait.

Our first summer in Harbor Country, I worked to ensure our guests' morning coffee at Camp Navama delivered not only caffeine but also a fantastic taste memory. One morning I woke up early to make coffee before the revelers rose. On the counter were packages of leftover gourmet marshmallows from the s'mores fest the night before. As I made my au lait with a dash of vanilla extract and nutmeg, I pondered: Why are marshmallows served with hot chocolate but never with coffee? Then I did what any mallow-loving lady would do and dropped two fluffy mocha chip marshmallows into the steaming hot, caffeinated cup. I walked down to the lake, mug in hand, sipping my favorite Infusco Coffee Roasters coffee through a smooth layer of mallow magic—and a new weekend ritual was born.

## Melting Mallow Café au Lait

**2** perfect morning servings   **10 min** start to finish

### SPECIAL ITEMS NEEDED
Milk frother

1 cup of your favorite freshly brewed coffee (I brew Infusco coffee, roasted in Sawyer, Michigan.)

1 teaspoon pure vanilla extract

2 teaspoons maple syrup (Use more or less to taste. In a pinch, use honey.)

1 cup hot frothed almond milk or milk of choice (I use refrigerated Elmhurst, Almond Breeze, or Califia Farms Barista Blend.)

4 gourmet marshmallows (Try Smashmallow or Hammond's.)

### TIPS FOR SUCCESS
*Not all dairy-free milk foams equally. For a thicker, creamier froth, I recommend refrigerated Almond Breeze Original Almondmilk, which is available at most markets.*

**Your Café au Lait Is Just Minutes Away!** Fill two of your favorite mugs half full with hot coffee. Split the vanilla, maple syrup, and frothed milk evenly between the mugs, then stir gently. Top each au lait with 2 marshmallows. Let the mallows melt for 1 minute or so to create a thin layer of mallow magic, making your morning coffee ritual that much sweeter.

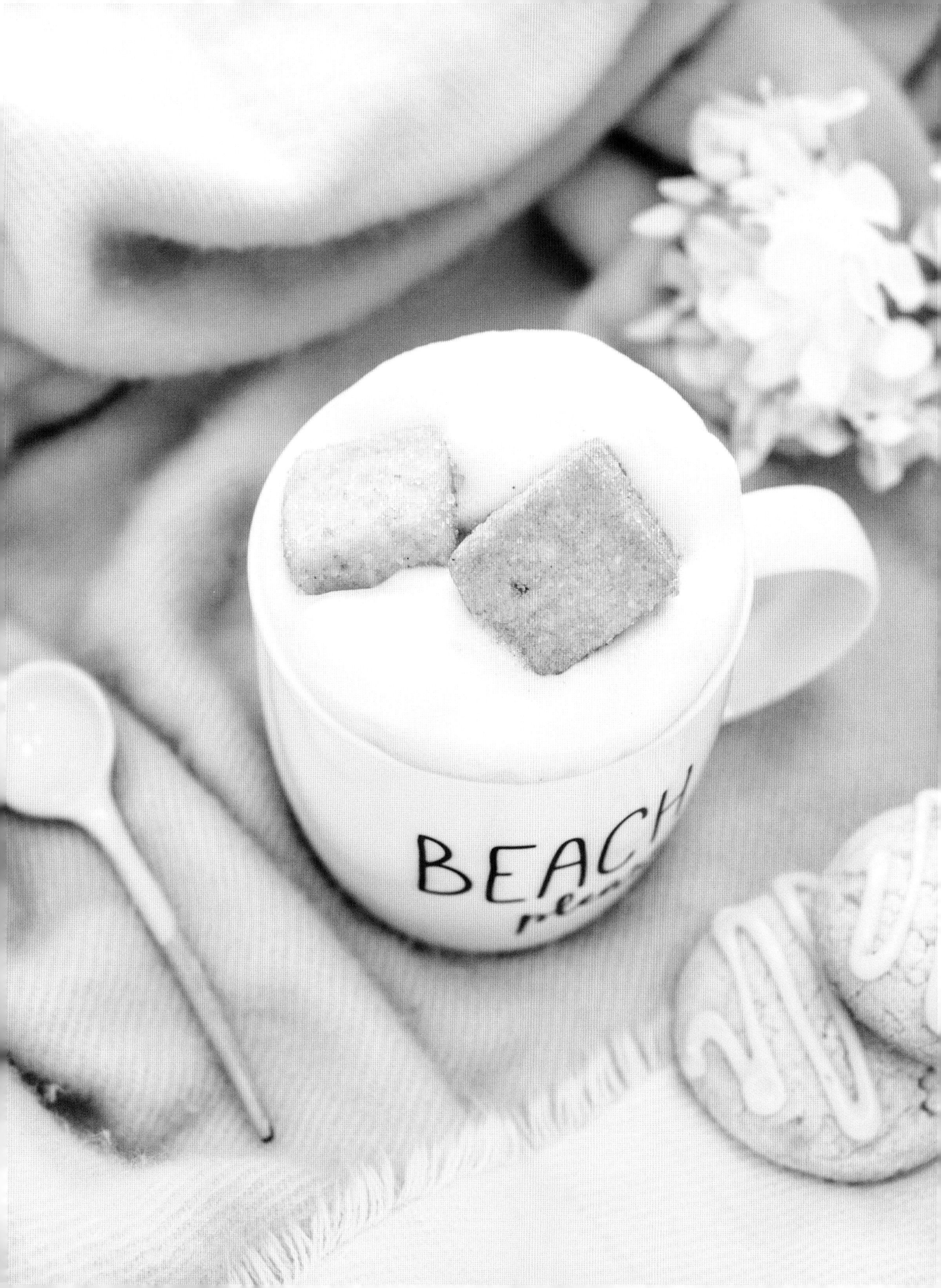
BEACH

"**B**UT FIRST, HOT CHOCOLATE." Despite being a full-grown adult, that became David's mantra when, in his late 20s, he realized he was allergic to COFFEE! Can you even imagine? Never one to dwell on a problem for too long, he quickly found a solution in the form of a homemade mug of "hot choccy" each morning.

His new ritual led me, ever the maximizer, to work on creating a delicious, dairy-free hot chocolate recipe, high in cocoa and lower in sugar. Before we discovered Harbor Country, I usually sweetened the pure cocoa powder with coconut sugar, but now I like using the bourbon barrel–aged maple syrup from Journeyman Distillery, located in the awesome little town of Three Oaks, Michigan. It turns out maple and chocolate love each other!

# Hubby's Hot Chocolate

**2** soul-warming servings    **10 min** start to finish

2 cups almond milk
or milk of choice

4 tablespoons unsweetened
cocoa powder

3 tablespoons maple syrup (Add
more or less to taste. In a pinch,
use agave or sugar of choice.)

1 teaspoon pure vanilla extract
(amps up the chocolate flavor)

⅛ teaspoon sea salt

4 cookie dough–flavored
marshmallows or mallows
of choice (Try Smashmallow
or Hammond's.)

**Simmer**  In a small pot, heat the milk over medium-high heat until simmering, but not boiling. Whisk as needed to prevent burning.

**Whisk**  Turn the heat to low and whisk in the cocoa powder, maple syrup, vanilla, and salt, stirring until the cocoa is dissolved and the mixture is smooth.

**Let's Drink!**  Pour the steaming hot chocolate into two ridiculously cozy mugs and top each with 2 cookie dough mallows . . . at least, that's the flavor the hubs always chooses. But you do you, boo.

### Freestyle

When the weather's warmer, this drink is delish over ice. In a small bowl or cup, whisk the cocoa powder with ½ cup hot milk until dissolved. Pour the cocoa milk into a small pitcher, add the remaining 1½ cups milk and the rest of the ingredients listed, and whisk to combine. Fill two glasses with ice and fill each with cocoa. *For this method you'll need to use maple syrup or agave, as honey and sugar won't dissolve in a cold liquid.*

Walking into the first annual Great Lakes Surf & Turf event at Flagship Specialty Foods and Fish Market, we were sidetracked by a table filled with small dark green glass bottles labeled "Fruitbelt." Endlessly curious about any new edible products, David and I were more than happy to take the vendors up on their offer to sample these curious tonics made with apple or cherry juice, bitters, honey, and a variety of botanicals. After one perfectly bubbly but not too sweet sip, I instantly knew these would become a staple offering at Camp Navama year-round. I also love that the name celebrates Southwest Michigan, a beloved part of America's fruit belt. Sip 'em solo or in a cocktail, or whip up one magical mocktail like this one, which drinks like a sparkling cherry lemonade. Cheers all around!

# Cherry Beach Fruitbelt Mocktail

🍸 **2** very-cherry servings    ⏱ **10 min** active time    ⧗ **6 hrs 10 min** start to finish

SPECIAL ITEMS NEEDED

Silicone ice cube trays with 1- or 2-inch cubes (I use silicone ice cube molds because they're pretty and the ice cubes melt more slowly. In a pinch, use regular ice cube trays.)

1 lemon

1½–2½ cups lemonade, divided

8 ounces Bright Cherry Fruitbelt, chilled

2 ounces soda water, chilled

3–4 dashes favorite bitters (optional; adds a tiny amount of alcohol)

**Make the Lemon Ice** Peel the rind from the lemon into ½-inch strips and place 1 or 2 pieces in each ice cube square. Fill the ice cube tray with 1 to 2 cups of the lemonade (depending on the size of the trays) and freeze for at least 6 hours or overnight. Chill glasses in the freezer if you're feeling fancy.

**Let's Drink!** Divide the remaining ½ cup lemonade, the Fruitbelt, the soda water, and the bitters (if using) equally between two glasses and stir. Add at least 1 lemonade ice cube to each glass. Serve immediately and enjoy living that zero-proof life.

> ### Freestyle
>
> Garnish with 2 fresh basil leaves, cut into thin strips.
>
> Make ice with your favorite juice instead of lemonade.
>
> Add ½ cup of your favorite rum or vodka to make this mocktail a cocktail!

The CHERRY BEACH FRUITBELT MOCKTAIL (page 162) we served guests old and young all summer long was a huge hit, so with cooler days on the horizon I wanted to replace the festive warm-weather drink with one that channeled all the cozy fall feelings. Harbor Country is located in one of America's most abundant fruit belts, so once peach, cherry, and berry season come to an end, u-pick lovers like me turn our attention to the endless apple orchards in Southwest Michigan. We already know caramel and apples are one dynamic duo, and combined with the warming flavors of ginger and clove plus a little sea salt, this mocktail makes colder days a lot easier to swallow!

# Salted Caramel Apple Mocktail with Fruitbelt

🍸 **2 tasty servings**   🕐 **15 min** active time   ⏳ **6 hrs 15 min** start to finish

SPECIAL ITEMS NEEDED

Silicone ice cube trays with 1- or 2-inch cubes (I use silicone ice cube molds because they're pretty and the ice cubes melt more slowly. In a pinch, use regular ice cube trays.)

1¼–2¼ cups apple cider, divided (In a pinch, use good apple juice.)

¼ cup caramel sauce

¼ cup kosher or sea salt

2 tablespoons diced apple, divided (Any apple variety will do.)

6 ounces Crisp Apple Fruitbelt, chilled

6 ounces ginger beer, chilled (I love Fever-Tree brand. In a pinch, use ginger ale.)

¼ cup apple cider, chilled (In a pinch, use good apple juice.)

Pinch ground cloves (optional but awesome)

**Make Ahead: Cider Ice**  Fill the ice cube tray with 1 to 2 cups of the apple cider (depending on the size of the trays) and freeze for at least 6 hours or overnight.

**Prep**  Pour the caramel sauce onto a small plate and the salt onto another small plate for rimming your glasses. Dip the glass rims into the caramel sauce, then the salt.

**Let's Drink!**  Fill the glasses with the cider ice cubes. Add 1 tablespoon of the diced apple to each glass. Divide the Fruitbelt, ginger beer, and remaining ¼ cup apple cider equally between the glasses, sprinkle with cloves (if using), and stir. Serve immediately and enjoy the warmer flavors of fall.

Y ES, THE SHEER NUMBER of u-pick farms was a huge draw for me when we decided to buy a home in Harbor Country. I will pick any fruit or vegetable any time, anywhere because it just makes me so freaking happy! Speaking of happy, we hosted many a happy hour at Camp Navama during our first New Buffalo summer, which inspired me to get crafty with my cocktails. The first time my mouth met a jalapeño-spiked margarita . . . fireworks! The heat ignites and excites the tequila while fresh fruit mellows everything out. For several summers watermelon was my go-to way to tame the flame, but once I discovered Michigan's super sweet u-pick blueberry scene, it was blueberry jalapeño margaritas for everyone, all summer long!

# Michigan Blueberry Jalapeño Margarita

🍸 **4** heat-seeker servings    🕐 **10 min** active time    ⧗ **6 hrs 10 min** start to finish

## SPECIAL ITEMS NEEDED

Muddler

Silicone ice cube trays with 1- or 2-inch cubes (I use silicone ice cube molds because they're pretty and the ice cubes melt more slowly. In a pinch, use regular ice cube trays.)

1–2 cups limeade

1 cup fresh blueberries, divided

1 jalapeño, divided

3 tablespoons agave (More or less to taste. In a pinch, use honey or simple syrup.)

2 cups regular ice

6 ounces tequila, chilled (I prefer reposado for a richer flavor, but blanco is also delicious.)

4 ounces soda water, chilled

2 ounces freshly squeezed lime juice (about 1–2 limes)

3 ounces limoncello (In a pinch, use Cointreau.)

## TIPS FOR SUCCESS

*Avoid touching your eyes after cutting the jalapeño and wash your hands with soap and olive oil to remove as much of the chile pepper goodness as possible!*

**Make the Limeade Ice** Fill the ice cube tray with the limeade, then add 2 to 3 blueberries to each cube. Freeze for at least 6 hours or overnight. Chill cocktail glasses of choice if you're feeling fancy.

**Prep the Jalapeño** Slice 8 thin rings off the tip of the jalapeño. Set aside for garnishing glasses. Slice the remaining jalapeño in half lengthwise and remove the seeds and white membrane using a small spoon. Slice the remaining jalapeño halves crosswise into thin pieces. Set aside.

**Let's Drink!** Fill each cocktail glass with limeade ice cubes, 1 tablespoon blueberries, and 2 rings of jalapeño. Set aside.

Add the remaining blueberries, about 2 tablespoons (more or less to taste) of the sliced jalapeño strips, and the agave to a cocktail shaker. Muddle well to crush the blueberries with the jalapeño and combine the agave. Add the regular ice, tequila, soda water, lime juice, and limoncello, then give a strong stir to combine. Strain into four glasses and toast to all the tequila-loving heat seekers.

### Freestyle

Swap out the blueberries for another fruit you think would pair well with heat, and muddle with one-quarter of a serrano pepper to make these margaritas a lotta hotta!

THERE'S NO BETTER PLACE than the lake for a five o'clock sip and smile soirée with close friends and family. One night we were invited to a dinner at Red Door Inn (a.k.a. RDI), home of our awesome friend Susan, who first opened our minds to the magic of Michigan when we saw her leave Chicago most weekends and escape to Harbor Country. When we arrived, everyone was drinking gin and tonics and David was treated to his very first G&T.

That night we discovered that not all tonic water is created equal. We'd never liked tonic until we experienced the superior flavor of Fever-Tree at the dinner party. It's not too bitter, not too sweet, and perfectly bubbly. Cheers to many happy cocktail hours filled with the spirit of Harbor Country!

# Summer Camp G&Ts with Grapefruit Ice Cubes

🍸 **2** refreshing servings    🕐 **10 min** active time    ⏳ **6 hrs 10 min** start to finish

## SPECIAL ITEMS NEEDED

Silicone ice cube trays with 1- or 2-inch cubes (I use silicone ice cube molds because they're pretty and the ice cubes melt more slowly. In a pinch, use regular ice cube trays.)

Coupe or martini glasses

---

6–12 lime peel twists

1½ cups grapefruit juice

¼ cup freshly squeezed lime juice

1 cup regular ice

5 ounces good tonic water, chilled (I love Fever-Tree Refreshingly Light.)

4 ounces gin or vodka, chilled (Try Journeyman Bilberry Black Hearts Gin or Journeyman Red Arrow Vodka.)

2 ounces soda water, chilled

Slices of cucumber, for garnish

## TIPS FOR SUCCESS
*Splurge on good tonic, girls and boys!*

**Make the Grapefruit Ice Cubes** Place 1 or 2 lime peel twists in each ice cube. In a small bowl, mix together the grapefruit and lime juices. Fill the ice cube mold with the juice mixture and freeze for at least 6 hours, until thoroughly frozen. Chill cocktail glasses if you're feeling fancy!

**Let's Drink!** Add the regular ice, tonic, gin, and soda water to a cocktail shaker. Give it a good stir.

Garnish each glass with 1 cucumber slice and fill with the grapefruit-lime ice cubes. Strain into two glasses and relax into this refreshingly delicious version of a classic summertime cocktail.

### Freestyle

Try Fever-Tree Sparkling Lemon in lieu of tonic and garnish with freshly ground black pepper.

Try Fever-Tree Ginger Beer in lieu of tonic and garnish with a slice of candied ginger.

You KNOW THOSE friends who become your chosen family members? For us, that's Kevin and Julie. This dynamic duo originally hails from Michigan, and they flew from California to Camp Navama for our very first New Buffalo Fourth of July!

Julie is known for her perfectly balanced, sweet-tart, pale pink Cosmopolitans, so I did what any Cosmo-loving gal pal would do and asked her to shake us up a few for magic hour, right before we joined the nightly neighborhood migration to the beach for sunset.

By the time the sun sank low, our Cosmo glow was in full effect! Because I care about how you sunset, I asked Julie to share her coveted Cosmo recipe.

# Lake Life Cranberry Limeade Cosmo

🍸 **1** perfect serving    🕐 **5 min** active time    ⧗ **25 min** start to finish

SPECIAL ITEMS NEEDED
Beach-friendly plastic wine or martini glass

3 ounces favorite vodka (I use Journeyman Red Arrow Vodka.)

1 ounce triple sec

2 ounces cranberry juice cocktail (Julie uses Ocean Spray.)

3 tablespoons limeade concentrate, thawed (Julie uses Minute Maid.)

Squeeze of fresh lime juice

TIPS FOR SUCCESS
*Sip and savor while watching the sun sink below the horizon or the kids and/or your significant other run wild through the sprinklers. Whatever your view, this cocktail will give it that Cosmo glow!*

**Chill** Chill a cocktail shaker and martini glass in the freezer for about 20 minutes.

**Shake** Add the vodka, triple sec, cranberry juice, and limeade concentrate to the chilled cocktail shaker. Shake your booty while you shake your Cosmo for about 10 seconds, because why not?!

**Let's Drink!** Strain into the chilled glass, add the fresh lime juice, sip, and smile!

# Secret Local Recipes

Part of what creates magical memories in places like Harbor Country are the local spots people visit again and again to connect over a shared meal, indulge in a slow brunch, or simply treat themselves to a dish that's become a family favorite.

During our first year at Camp Navama, we enjoyed discovering our own favorite places for epic breakfasts, perfect lunches after long bike rides, and delicious dinners. In writing this book, I wanted to give people the chance to take a piece of this special community home through some of the incredible food made in Harbor Country's best kitchens.

This collection of coveted recipes includes the locally famous buckwheat crepes from Luisa's Café and Harbert Swedish Bakery (page 176), Whistle Stop Asian Noodle Salad (page 184), which is perfect for the beach, Red Arrow Roadhouse Gumbo (page 206), Terrace Room Fettuccine al Pomodoro (page 198), Flagship Grilled Sturgeon with Citrus Vinaigrette (page 202), and many more! Thanks to the generous people willing to contribute a few of their prized recipes, now you can experience the delicious flavors of Harbor Country, no matter where your kitchen might be.

# Love at First (Swedish) Bite

THERE ARE SOME places I like to eat and others that fall into the true love category. **Luisa's Café** and the attached **Harbert Swedish Bakery** captured my heart early in our Harbor Country adventure days. I discovered they not only make sublime pecan sticky buns and use my favorite almond milk for lattes but also serve up glorious gluten-free goodness like their famous crustless quiche, lemon rosemary scones, and Swedish buckwheat pancakes!

Current owners Luisa and Vivian are a talented mother and daughter duo who continually deliver delicious food to loyal fans and newcomers alike. They cook and bake with their hearts, and you can taste the love in every single bite.

The sweet and savory crepe recipes contributed for this book are served at Luisa's Café for special occasions. Thankfully, you can now sleep well at night knowing these legendary buckwheat crepes are in your very own recipe wheelhouse, ready to be whipped up whenever and wherever, for anyone lucky enough to share them with you!

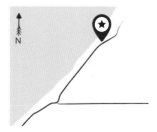

### ★ Luisa's Café and Harbert Swedish Bakery

13698 Red Arrow Hwy. | Harbert, MI

Both sweet and savory cravings can be met from the wide variety of menu offerings at Luisa's Café, including French lentils with eggs, Dutch apple pancakes, chilaquiles, and baked quinoa with cardamom and almond milk. Make sure to stop by the Harbert Swedish Bakery to take home any of the indulgent pastries, life-changing cookies, or a truly memorable gluten-free scone.

# Luisa's Café Blueberry Mascarpone Crepes

**¶1 4–6** heavenly servings    ⏳ **1 hr 30 min** start to finish

Contributed by Luisa Mills and Vivian May, Luisa's Café and Harbert Swedish Bakery

## SPECIAL ITEMS NEEDED

8-inch nonstick oven-safe skillet or crepe pan

## MASCARPONE FILLING

8 ounces cream cheese, softened

4 ounces mascarpone cheese, very slightly softened (don't microwave)

2 tablespoons confectioners' sugar

1 teaspoon lemon zest

## BLUEBERRY SAUCE

½ cup freshly squeezed orange juice

Zest and juice of 1 lemon

2 tablespoons potato starch

2 tablespoons granulated sugar

2 cups fresh or frozen blueberries, divided

2 tablespoons Grand Marnier

## WHIPPED CREAM

1 cup very cold heavy cream

## BUCKWHEAT SWEDISH CREPES

¼ cup plus 2 tablespoons potato starch

¼ cup plus 2 tablespoons buckwheat flour

1 teaspoon sea salt

3 eggs, beaten

1 cup whole milk, divided

1½ tablespoons unsalted butter, melted and cooled, plus more for cooking crepes

1 teaspoon pure vanilla extract

Confectioners' sugar, for garnish

Fresh blueberries, for garnish

## TIPS FOR SUCCESS

*If the crepes bubble, your pan is too hot. Reduce the heat slightly to ensure a flat, even crepe.*

*The mascarpone filling and blueberry sauce can be made 1 day ahead. Bring to room temperature before using.*

**Make the Mascarpone Filling** In a medium bowl using an electric handheld mixer or a standing mixer fit with the paddle attachment, beat the cream cheese into a soft cream. Add the mascarpone, confectioners' sugar, and lemon zest and mix on medium speed until smooth, about 1 minute. Do not overbeat. Cover and set aside or refrigerate if not using right away.

**Make the Blueberry Sauce** Put the orange juice, lemon zest and juice, potato starch, and sugar into a medium saucepan. Whisk thoroughly. Over medium heat, cook until thickened, whisking constantly so the potato starch doesn't get lumpy. Add ½ cup of the blueberries and cook until softened, about 5 minutes. Remove from the heat and add the remaining 1½ cups of blueberries and the Grand Marnier. Stir to combine, then let rest to thicken and cool.

**Make the Whipped Cream** In a medium bowl using an electric handheld mixer or a standing mixer fit with the whisk attachment, whip the very cold cream on medium to medium-high speed until stiff peaks form. Store in an airtight container in the refrigerator until ready to use. Whip again if needed before using.

**Make the Crepe Batter** In a medium bowl, whisk together the potato starch, buckwheat flour, and salt. Add the eggs and ½ cup of the milk and whisk until smooth. The batter should be pourable. Add the remaining ½ cup of milk, the melted butter, and the vanilla. Whisk again until smooth.

**Cook the Crepes** Heat a heavy 8-inch nonstick skillet over medium-high heat. Coat the pan with a little butter. Ladle about ⅓ cup of the batter into the pan, tilting the pan gently to spread the batter evenly. Let cook until the batter is not runny and the bottom is brown. Run a rubber spatula along the edges of the crepe to loosen. Using a spatula or butter knife, flip the crepe over to cook for about 1 minute on the other side. Once done, place on a baking sheet and set aside to cool. Repeat with the remaining batter, stirring as needed.

**Fill and Bake the Crepes** Preheat the oven to 375°F. Line up the cooled crepes on a flat surface. Put ¼ cup of the mascarpone filling on the top left side of each crepe. Fold in half to cover the filling, then in half again to make a triangle.

Heat butter in the bottom of a heavy nonstick oven-safe skillet over medium heat. (Use the same 8-inch skillet the crepes were made in if it's oven-safe.) Working in batches, place the crepes in the pan and cook on the stovetop for about 1 minute, or until lightly browned. Flip the crepes in the pan, then place them in the oven for about 5 minutes, or until heated through.

**Let's Eat!** Spoon blueberry sauce onto each plate, nestle 1 to 2 crepes on top, and garnish with fresh whipped cream, a sprinkle of confectioners' sugar, and fresh blueberries. Relish the moment. It's delicious.

# Luisa's Café Goat Cheese Crepe Pillows

**¶ 4–6** scrumptious servings　　🕐 **1 hr 30 min** active time　　⏳ **2 hrs** start to finish

Contributed by Luisa Mills and Vivian May, Luisa's Café and Harbert Swedish Bakery

## SPECIAL ITEMS NEEDED

8-inch nonstick oven-safe skillet or crepe pan

## GOAT CHEESE FILLING

8 ounces cream cheese, softened

8 ounces goat cheese, softened

2 cloves roasted garlic, smashed (see Tips for Success box)

Pinch of sea salt and freshly ground black pepper

2 fresh basil leaves, thinly sliced

2 tablespoons thinly sliced sundried tomatoes

## BUCKWHEAT SWEDISH CREPES

¼ cup plus 2 tablespoons potato starch

¼ cup plus 2 tablespoons buckwheat flour

1 teaspoon sea salt

3 eggs, beaten

1 cup whole milk, divided

1½ tablespoons unsalted butter, melted and cooled, plus more for cooking crepes

1 teaspoon pure vanilla extract

Grated Asiago cheese, for garnish

## TOMATO SAUCE

2 tablespoons olive oil

1 (28-ounce) can diced San Marzano tomatoes

Pinch of sea salt and freshly ground black pepper, to taste

## SPINACH

1 tablespoon olive oil

2 cups fresh spinach

## TIPS FOR SUCCESS

*If the crepes bubble, your pan is too hot.*

### HOW TO ROAST GARLIC

*Preheat the oven to 400°F. Remove the skin from a garlic head. Slice off the top portion of the garlic head to expose the garlic cloves. Place the garlic in the center of a sheet of aluminum foil, 8 to 10 inches long. Drizzle with 2 tablespoons olive oil. Wrap the garlic head in the foil. Place in the oven and roast for 35 to 45 minutes, until soft. Let cool slightly.*

**Make the Goat Cheese Filling** In a medium bowl using an electric handheld mixer or a standing mixer fit with the paddle attachment, beat the cream cheese into a soft cream. Add the goat cheese, garlic, salt, and pepper. Beat until well combined. Mix in the basil and sundried tomatoes with a spatula. Cover and set aside, or refrigerate if not using right away.

**Make the Crepe Batter** In a medium bowl, whisk together the potato starch, buckwheat flour, and salt. Add the eggs and ½ cup of the milk and whisk until smooth. The batter should be pourable. Add the remaining ½ cup of milk, the melted butter, and the vanilla. Whisk again until smooth.

**Cook the Crepes** Heat a heavy 8-inch nonstick skillet over medium-high heat. Coat the pan with a little butter. Ladle about ⅓ cup of the batter in the pan, tilting the pan gently to spread the batter evenly. Let cook until the batter is not runny and the bottom is brown. Run a rubber spatula along the edges of the crepe to loosen. Using a spatula or butter knife, flip the crepe over to cook for about 1 minute on the other side. Once done, place on a baking sheet and set aside to cool. Repeat with the remaining batter, stirring as needed.

**Make the Tomato Sauce** In a medium sauté pan, heat the olive oil over medium heat. Turn the flame to low and add the tomatoes, salt, and pepper. Simmer until some of the liquid evaporates, about 30 minutes. Remove from the heat and set aside.

**Sauté the Spinach** In a medium sauté pan, heat the olive oil. Add the spinach and cook over medium heat until just wilted, about 3 minutes. Set aside.

**Fill and Bake the Crepes** Preheat the oven to 375°F. Line up the cooled crepes on a flat surface. Put ¼ cup of the goat cheese filling on the top left side of each crepe. Fold in half to cover the filling, then in half again to make a triangle.

Heat butter in the bottom of a heavy, nonstick oven-safe skillet over medium heat. (Use the same 8-inch skillet the crepes were made in if it's oven-safe.) Working in batches, place the crepes in the pan and cook on the stovetop for about 1 minute, or until lightly browned. Flip the crepes in the pan and place them in the oven for about 5 minutes, or until heated through.

**Let's Eat!** Bring the tomato sauce back to a simmer while the crepes cook in the oven. Ladle ½ cup of the warm tomato sauce onto each plate. Nestle 1 to 2 crepes on the sauce, top with spinach, and sprinkle with Asiago cheese. Serve hot.

# Can Ya' Hear the Whistle Blowin'?

WHEN I GO TO **Whistle Stop Grocery**, I'm hungry for happy. Delicious happiness, delivered in the form of great coffee, craveable kale salad, fancy-schmancy crackers, gourmet condiments, swoon-worthy pastries, the best orange marmalade ever, or a large slice of whatever whimsical cake is gracing the pastry case that week—such as strawberry rosé or blueberry pancake cake. Yes, they're impossible to resist, so don't even try. Just grab a friend and a fork and enjoy!

Luckily for all of us, the Whistle team agreed to share two recipes, one sweet, one savory, both sure to become fast family favorites! The glorious Aunt Wilma Bars (page 188) appear once the weather warms and make an easy-to-eat treat beachside or at a BBQ, while the always popular Asian Noodle Salad (page 184) will never fail to impress your guests.

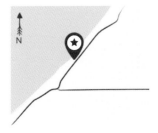

### ★ Whistle Stop Grocery

**15700 Red Arrow Hwy. | Union Pier, MI**

A Whistle Stop customer captured my feelings about this little gourmet market perfectly in a painting (displayed in the shop) depicting a girl with a sad face "before Whistle" and a happy grin "after Whistle!" Whether I pop in mid-run for a café au lait or grab a much-needed lunch after a long countryside bike ride, this exquisitely curated wonderland of sweets and treats never fails to bring a smile to my face. So the next time you wake up in Harbor Country looking for happiness, walk, run, bike, or drive to Whistle Stop!

# Whistle Stop Asian Noodle Salad

**4–6** addictive servings      **45 min** start to finish                     Contributed by Whistle Stop Grocery and Chef Eva Frahm

1 pound angel hair or capellini pasta (Use De Cecco brand, if available.)

5 ounces shiitake mushrooms, stemmed and thinly sliced (Use more, if preferred.)

¼ cup plus ⅓ cup extra virgin olive oil, divided

¾ teaspoon kosher salt, divided

½ teaspoon freshly ground black pepper, divided

¾ cup hoisin sauce, divided

1 medium red bell pepper (Use more, if preferred.)

1 medium yellow bell pepper (Use more, if preferred.)

¼ cup seasoned rice wine vinegar

1 tablespoon garlic chili sauce

Sriracha, to taste (optional)

4 scallions, thinly sliced

1 cup lightly packed cilantro leaves, chopped

**Cook the Noodles**  Bring a large pot of water to a boil. Salt the pasta water, if desired. Add the angel hair and cook 7 to 8 minutes until just al dente, so the noodles are still slightly firm and not overcooked. Drain into a colander, rinse gently with cold water, let drain again, then place in a large bowl. Set aside.

**Prep the Vegetables and Sauce**  In a skillet over medium heat, sauté the mushrooms in ¼ cup of the olive oil for about 7 minutes, or until lightly browned. Season with ⅛ teaspoon of the salt and ⅛ teaspoon of the pepper. Remove from the heat and add 2 tablespoons of the hoisin sauce. Stir to coat and set aside.

Julienne the bell peppers by cutting them into ⅛-inch-thick strips. Set aside.

In a small mixing bowl, whisk together the remaining 10 tablespoons hoisin sauce, the remaining ⅓ cup olive oil, the rice vinegar, the garlic chili sauce, and the Sriracha (if using). Set aside.

Add the mushrooms, peppers, scallions, cilantro, and sauce mixture to the noodles.

Toss gently to incorporate. Season to taste with the remaining salt and the remaining pepper and transfer to a serving bowl or store covered in the refrigerator for 5 to 7 days.

**Let's Eat!**  This is one of my favorite recipes to bring to the beach packed in individual takeaway boxes with chopsticks for everyone.

"This recipe is a Whistle Stop best seller. It is great served cold or at room temp for a lighter lunch or dinner, or great to take along to the beach or a summer picnic. The flavors are fresh, and you can adjust the heat if you prefer something a little more spicy by adding Sriracha."
—*Whistle Stop Grocery team*

# Whistle Stop Aunt Wilma Bar

🍴 **20–24** craveable servings  🕐 **30 min** active time  ⧗ **2 hrs** start to finish

Contributed by Whistle Stop Grocery, Chef Kelsey Morgan, and Aunt Wilma

2 cups sweetened shredded coconut

1 cup chopped pecans

1 cup (2 sticks) unsalted butter

2 cups graham cracker crumbs

½ teaspoon kosher salt

1 cup dark chocolate chips (Semisweet work great too!)

1 cup butterscotch chips

2 (14-ounce) cans sweetened condensed milk

Sea salt, for garnish

"The Aunt Wilma bars were made regularly for family gatherings. She combined graham cracker crust, toasted coconut, toasted pecans, chocolate, and butterscotch to make her bars. Not only is it truly delicious—it is something everyone has come to love. Chewy, sweet, salty goodness!" —*Whistle Stop Grocery team*

TIPS FOR SUCCESS

*Use a soft coconut, like Baker's Angel Flake, to achieve the right bar texture and flavor.*

**Prep**  Preheat the oven to 325°F. Set aside two baking sheets.

Grease a 9 × 13-inch baking pan and line it with parchment paper so that all the sides are covered. Leave approximately 1 inch of the parchment paper hanging over the edges of your pan. This will make it so much easier to release the bar later!

**Toast the Coconut**  Spread the coconut on one of the baking sheets in an even layer and toast for 5 to 8 minutes, until lightly golden brown. Remove and let cool.

**Toast the Pecans**  Spread the chopped pecans on the other baking sheet in an even layer and toast for 5 to 8 minutes, until fragrant. Remove and let cool.

**Brown the Butter**  On the stovetop, heat the butter in a small saucepan over medium heat, whisking often, until it browns, dark speckles appear, and you smell a wonderful nutty fragrance. This should take about 5 to 7 minutes. Remove from the heat and let cool slightly. *Special Note: Butter burns easily, so watch carefully.*

**Make and Bake the Crust**  In a medium mixing bowl, combine the graham cracker crumbs with the brown butter and kosher salt. Press this mixture into the bottom of the prepared baking pan. Hard pack the graham cracker crumbs to ensure the crust stays intact when the bars are cut. Bake at 325°F for 10 to 15 minutes, until the crust is an even golden brown. Remove from the oven and allow the crust to cool completely before cutting.

**Make the Bar Layers**  Evenly layer the toasted coconut, chocolate chips, butterscotch chips, and pecans over the crust. Use the back of a large spoon or spatula to evenly distribute the sweetened condensed milk as you pour it over the dry ingredients. Lightly sprinkle sea salt over the entire bar.

**Bake the Bar**  Bake at 325°F for 50 to 60 minutes. The finished bar should be evenly brown and bubbly! Remove from the oven and let cool completely.

**Let's Eat!**  Use a butter knife to separate the baked bar from the sides of the pan. Once all the sides have been freed, gently tug on the parchment paper to release the bar. Place the bar on a cutting board and use a sharp chef's knife to cut as desired.

The bars can be kept in an airtight container in the refrigerator for up to 2 weeks. Aunt Wilma Bars are best served at room temperature. They are more ooey-gooey that way!

# Chili Me Silly

I T WAS THE dead of winter in Harbor Country, and we were hungry for anything hearty. Roasts, stews, and thick slices of richly buttered bread all become alluring when temperatures linger below 30 degrees for many months.

One bone-chillingly cold afternoon, we wandered into **David's Delicatessen** looking for a place to warm up and get some work done. Normally David would have ordered the grass-fed beef chili, but after the New Year he had turned to a more plant-based diet. We tucked into two steaming bowls of the vegan chili. It was smoky and sweet with a perfect heat, and wow, was it hearty! Week after week we returned to enjoy bowl after bowl. One day I heard another customer describe it as "soul-changing chili," and I was glad to know we weren't the only ones who were obsessed. Thankfully delicatessen owners Emma Brewster and Joe Lindsay, along with chili creator Stacey MacGregor, were willing to share this incredibly awesome recipe.

When Stacey gave me the recipe, however, it came with a caveat. She doesn't really cook with recipes, so she didn't know exactly how much of each ingredient went into a pot of her magical chili. But she did know that no two versions were ever totally the same. I whipped up a few batches to have Stacey and team taste. They said this recipe comes very close, but to get a bowl of the original, you'll just have to visit David's in the winter, when the weather's cold, the town is calm, and you're hungry for something hearty!

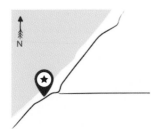

★ David's Delicatessen

30 N. Whittaker St. | New Buffalo, MI

David's Delicatessen is a New Buffalo favorite, known far and wide for its epic sandwiches. David's offers a variety of Reuben sandwiches, breakfast sandwiches, and incredibly creative vegan sandwich options as well.

# David's Delicatessen Vegan Chili

🍴 **10–12** soul-soothing servings    🕐 **1 hr** active time    ⏳ **2 hrs 30 min** start to finish     Contributed by Stacey MacGregor, David's Delicatessen

6 cups peeled and cubed sweet potatoes (about 3 small or 2 large sweet potatoes)

3 cups peeled and chopped red onions (about 1½ large red onions)

2 cups peeled and chopped carrots (about 3 large or 4 medium carrots)

2 cups seeded and chopped bell peppers (about 2 large bell peppers of any color)

2 cups diced celery

2 cloves garlic, peeled and crushed

½ cup olive oil

¼ cup plus 2 tablespoons good chili powder, plus more to taste

1 tablespoon plus 2 teaspoons ground cumin, plus more to taste

2 teaspoons fennel seeds, plus more to taste (optional, but Stacey uses them!)

1 tablespoon kosher salt, plus more to taste

2 (28-ounce) cans diced or chopped tomatoes, including liquid

1 cup water (more or less as needed for desired chili consistency)

1 teaspoon red pepper flakes, plus more to taste (optional)

3 (15-ounce) cans beans with liquid (I use a combination of black, pinto, and kidney or navy. Choose whatever beans float your boat!)

TIPS FOR SUCCESS

*The sweet potatoes don't need to be perfect cubes, but should be fairly consistent in size (about ½ inch each) so they cook evenly.*

*Chop the onions, carrots, peppers, and celery to be similar in size but a bit smaller than the sweet potato pieces.*

*The flavor of the chili changes and the heat mellows out in the days after it's made, so taste and adjust the spice to your liking.*

**Prep** Preheat the oven to 350°F. Position the oven racks in the upper and lower thirds of the oven. Line two baking sheets with aluminum foil or parchment paper and set aside.

**Combine the Veggies** Place the sweet potato cubes, onions, carrots, bell peppers, and celery into a large mixing bowl. Add the crushed garlic and stir to combine.

**Season the Veggies** If needed, divide the veggie medley into two bowls so you have enough room to toss with the olive oil and spices.

Drizzle the veggies with the olive oil and toss to coat well. Add the chili powder and again toss to coat well. Add the cumin powder, fennel seeds (if using), and salt. These spices can all be adjusted to taste later. Toss again and spread all these goodies out on the prepared baking sheets in an even layer.

**Bake the Veggies** Bake the veggies for about 50 to 60 minutes, until the sweet potatoes are tender. Rotate the pans halfway through baking to cook evenly. *Special Note: You can bump up the heat to 375°F or even 400°F if you're short on time and need them to cook faster.*

**Make the Chili** Transfer the roasted veggies to a large kettle or soup pot and add the canned tomatoes and enough water to reach chili consistency—not too thick, not too watery—"chili-like." Now the fun part: taste, adjust your seasonings if need be, and add the red pepper flakes (if using). Add the beans and stir to combine.

Put the pot on the stove over medium-high heat and simmer slowly for at least 1 hour, adding more water if needed. Stir, taste, and adjust the seasonings as needed as the flavors meld. Voilà!

**Let's Eat!** Serve this hearty vegan chili in large mugs or deep bowls when the cold weather comes calling. It's delicious served with my Cornbread Leek Muffins (page 88). This chili can be refrigerated in an airtight container for 4 to 5 days or frozen for up to 3 months.

# Dinner for Two with a View

O UR FIRST SUMMER in Harbor Country, Camp Navama became an impromptu B&B, and we loved every minute of it. Hosting all the friends and family we could gather for sleepover weekends, complete with pre-paddleboarding breakfasts and long, casual alfresco dinners, created a season of delicious memories. But I must admit that when the first guest-free weekend rolled around, I told David the kitchen was closed and we'd be going out for dinner.

The Jollys, our most festive New Buffalo friends, were always raving about **Bentwood Tavern**, so we booked a reservation. At the **Marina Grand Resort**, where Bentwood Tavern is located, we walked into a modern-meets-nautical lounge area and were more than happy to enjoy a cocktail while waiting for a table on the patio. Once seated with a view of the marina, we relaxed into the night and perused the eclectic menu. There's something for whatever you're craving, whether it's the vibrant Green Rice Bowl (page 196), grilled Mexican street corn, flown-in fresh fish, or Corporate Chef Jenny Drilon's legendary Bangkok chicken.

A few weeks later it was high time for a girls' night out, so my friend Amy and I treated ourselves to dinner and vino at the **Terrace Room**, Bentwood's Italian sister restaurant tucked inside **The Harbor Grand Hotel**. Executive Chef Alberto Ilescas creates authentic rustic Italian fare with suave flair in an elegantly cozy atmosphere.

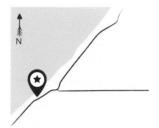

★ Bentwood Tavern at the Marina Grand Resort

600 W. Water St. | New Buffalo, MI

★ Terrace Room at The Harbor Grand Hotel

111 W. Water St. | New Buffalo, MI

There are many reasons to return to Bentwood Tavern often for dinner, brunch, lunch, taco night, sushi night—and of course for the fantastic seasonal cocktails! With warm weather, dine alfresco at the Terrace Room over a gorgeous plate of freshly made pasta, which thankfully you can now prepare at home to impress your guests, your honey, or just yourself!

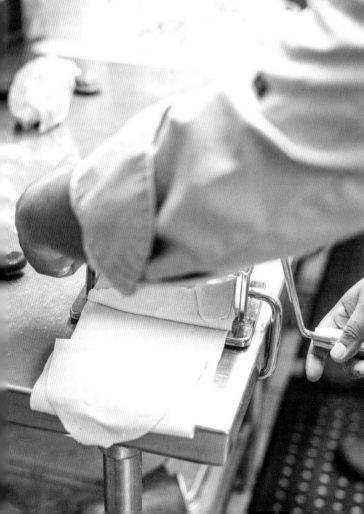

# Bentwood Tavern Green Rice Bowl

**4–6** satisfying servings    **1 hr 30 min** start to finish    Contributed by Corporate Chef Jenny Drilon, Bentwood Tavern and Terrace Room

## CUBAN BLACK BEANS

½ poblano pepper

2 tablespoons olive oil

¼ large Spanish (yellow) onion, diced in ¼-inch pieces

½ fresh jalapeño, finely diced

1 teaspoon smoked Spanish paprika, plus more to taste

½ teaspoon freshly ground black pepper, plus more to taste

1 teaspoon minced garlic

1½ teaspoons kosher salt, plus more to taste

2 (15-ounce) cans black beans with liquid

## GREEN RICE

½ teaspoon kosher salt

2 tablespoons vegetable base (Better Than Bouillon brand or homemade)

2½ cups water

1½ cups lightly packed spinach

½ cup lightly packed cilantro leaves

1 jalapeño, stemmed

1 shallot, root end removed and peeled

1 clove garlic

1½ cups brown rice

3 tablespoons olive oil

## ROASTED SWEET POTATO ROUNDS

2 pounds sweet potatoes, peeled and cut into ½-inch rounds

2 tablespoons olive oil

1 teaspoon smoked Spanish paprika

½ teaspoon kosher salt

## KALE

1 tablespoon olive oil

6 cups torn stemmed Tuscan kale (about 2-inch pieces)

Salt and freshly ground black pepper, to taste

**Prepare the Cuban Black Beans** Using cooking tongs, hold the poblano pepper half over the stovetop or an open flame on the oven burner until blackened. Remove from the heat and let cool briefly. Peel off the black portions and dice into ¼-inch pieces. Add the olive oil to a medium saucepan. Over medium heat, sauté the pepper, onion, jalapeño, paprika, black pepper, and garlic until the vegetables are soft but not browned, seasoning with the salt.

Drain the water from the cans of beans, reserving a little of the liquid in a small bowl, and add the beans to the saucepan. Stir and simmer for about 20 minutes on medium-low heat, adding water from the cans of beans as needed if the beans get dry. Check the seasoning and adjust to taste. The Cuban beans may be made 2 days ahead. Keep refrigerated in an airtight container until needed, then warm.

**Prepare the Green Rice** Add the salt, vegetable base, water, spinach, cilantro, jalapeño, shallot, and garlic to a blender and blend until smooth. Set aside. In a 2-quart saucepan with a lid, sauté the brown rice with the olive oil over medium heat for 4 to 6 minutes. Add the green mixture to the rice, cover with the lid, and simmer on low heat for 25 to 35 minutes. Do not stir until the liquid is gone and the rice is tender. (This may also be done in a rice cooker.) Stir well when the rice is done.

**Roast the Sweet Potato Rounds** Preheat the oven to 400°F. Toss the sweet potatoes with the olive oil in a large bowl or directly on a baking sheet. Place the rounds in a single layer on a baking sheet, sprinkle with the paprika and salt, and roast at 400°F for 10 to 20 minutes, until the potatoes are soft and cooked through. Remove from the oven and set aside.

**Sauté the Kale** Pour the olive oil in a large skillet and sauté the kale over medium heat until wilted, 3 to 5 minutes. Season with salt and pepper to taste. Set aside.

**Let's Eat!** Use four to six deep "entrée-size" bowls and add approximately ¾ cup of the hot Cuban beans to one side of each bowl. Add about 1 cup of the green rice to the opposite side of the bowl. Layer about 5 sweet potato rounds on the top on one side, then add the wilted kale (dividing the kale evenly among the bowls). You can serve this with diced avocado, a sprinkle of roasted pepitas and queso fresco cubes, and your favorite tomatillo sauce.

# Terrace Room Fettuccine al Pomodoro

**¶¶ 4** delizioso servings    ◷ **1 hr** active time    ⧗ **1 hr 30 min** start to finish

Contributed by Executive Chef Alberto Ilescas, Bentwood Tavern and Terrace Room

SPECIAL ITEMS NEEDED

Pasta machine with roller for fettuccine

PASTA

2¼ cups 00 flour

4 eggs

¼ cup plus 1 teaspoon kosher salt, divided

¼ teaspoon freshly ground black pepper

1 gallon water

TOMATO SAUCE

2 tablespoons peeled and diced shallot

1 tablespoon minced garlic

1 tablespoon extra virgin olive oil

1 (28-ounce) can whole San Marzano tomatoes with juice

Kosher salt and freshly ground black pepper, to taste

2 ounces fresh basil, thinly sliced, for garnish

3 ounces grated Parmigiano-Reggiano, for garnish

TIPS FOR SUCCESS

*The 00 flour is critical for the success of this pasta. You can easily order it online if it's not available locally. King Arthur Italian-Style Flour can be used in a pinch. The term "00 flour" (pronounced "double zero flour" and also called doppio zero) typically refers to Italian milled flour used for making pasta. This flour is graded 2, 1, 0, or 00. This indicates how finely the flour has been ground, with 2 being the most coarse and 00 being powder fine.*

**Make the Pasta Dough**  Place the flour in a mound on a flat surface and create a well in the center large enough to hold 4 eggs. Break the eggs into the middle of the well, add 1 teaspoon of the salt and the pepper, and break the egg yolks with the tips of your fingers, pulling in the flour from the sides of the well as you go to incorporate it at the same time. (The dough will be sticky, then shaggy, but will eventually come together with a little patience.) Once a semisolid dough forms, knead for 7 to 10 minutes. Wrap the pasta dough in plastic wrap and let it rest for 30 minutes at room temperature.

Unwrap the dough and place on a floured work surface. Cut the dough into 4 equal pieces. With a roller on the thickest roller gauge to begin, feed the dough through the flat rollers of a pasta machine. Feed in the pasta sheet with one hand and turn the handle quickly with the other to ensure the dough rolls out evenly.

Fold the pasta sheet in half, bringing the long ends of the sheet together, and feed again through the machine. Continue to fold in half until the width of the dough matches the width of the pasta opening in the machine, trimming the sides with a knife as needed. Once the widths match, turn the pasta machine down 1 gauge and roll the dough through. Continue this process *without folding again* until the pasta is the desired thickness, going down 1 gauge each time on the machine. The pasta should be rolled until it is a little less than ¼ inch thick.

Once the proper thickness is reached, using a fettuccini roller, cut the rolled dough into ribbons about 10 inches long and ¼ inch wide. Carefully separate the pasta ribbons and spread out on a lightly floured baking sheet before boiling. You can also hang the pasta on a pasta drying rack, if preferred.

Combine the water and the remaining ¼ cup of salt in a large pot over high heat and bring to a boil.

**Make the Tomato Sauce**  While the pasta water comes to a boil, make the sauce. In a large pan over medium heat, lightly sauté the shallot and garlic with the olive oil until the shallot is translucent. Add the tomatoes, salt, and pepper and cook for 5 to 10 minutes. Crush the whole tomatoes as needed with a spoon in the pan.

**Boil the Pasta and Add to the Sauce**  Put the fresh pasta in the pot of boiling water for 90 seconds. Then drain the excess water and add the pasta to the pan with the tomato sauce. Toss well to coat. Remove from the heat.

**Let's Eat!**  Divide the pasta into four serving bowls. Garnish each with the basil and cheese. Serve while piping hot and enjoy every freshly made bite.

# Salute the Flagship

**W**E NEARLY WALKED away from closing on our New Buffalo home. A few inconvenient realities about the property had come to light that gave us pause, and we felt torn about the path forward. Then, in early May, we received a sign in the form of a fish.

We'd driven by the cottage-cute **Flagship Specialty Foods and Fish Market** on Red Arrow Highway numerous times while house hunting, but on this day in May we stopped to check it out. Inside the quaint little shop, we carefully studied the scrawled chalkboard that listed everything fresh for the day and admired the array of offerings, ranging from a crispy golden porchetta to crab cakes to fresh fish-and-chips!

I got to chatting with chef and owner Rachel Collins about our potential move to Harbor Country. She told us, "Oh, you guys should come to this charity event I'm hosting next weekend with a whole local Mangalitsa hog and roast sturgeon!"

Neither David nor I had ever heard of sturgeon, let alone eaten the prehistoric-looking fish, but we couldn't ignore the fact that the home we were trying to buy just happened to be located in Sturgeon Beach. The event was nearly sold out, but Rachel found a way to secure two more tickets for us.

The event also gave us a glimpse into the world we were hoping to find in Harbor Country, where time slows down, people are present, and neighbors still share sugar. We left the Sunday gathering with full bellies and satisfied souls knowing we'd met Rachel for a reason.

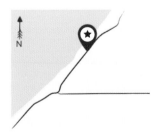

### ★ Flagship Specialty Foods and Fish Market

14939 Red Arrow Hwy. | Lakeside, MI

Thanks to Flagship Specialty Foods and Fish Market, I have year-round access to fresh, gorgeous seafood despite our rural address. Proprietor Rachel Collins procures top-quality ingredients, and special orders can be made with advance notice. The Faroe Islands salmon is consistently amazing, and don't miss out on specialties like porchetta, candied salmon, and some of the best baguettes outside Paris.

# Flagship Grilled Sturgeon with Citrus Vinaigrette

🍴 **6–8** spectacular servings  🕐 **1 hr** active time  ⏳ **4 hrs** start to finish

Contributed by Principal and Chef Rachel Collins, Flagship Specialty Foods and Fish Market

## STURGEON

3–4 pounds sturgeon, in one piece (Sturgeon is typically available seasonally at Flagship Specialty Foods and Fish Market, but call ahead to check or custom order.)

¼ cup plus 2 tablespoons olive oil, divided

3 tablespoons kosher salt, plus more to taste

Freshly ground black pepper, to taste

2 medium navel oranges, cut into ½-inch slices

## CITRUS VINAIGRETTE

1 egg yolk

¼ cup orange juice

¼ cup apple cider vinegar

1 tablespoon orange zest

1 tablespoon lemon zest

1 tablespoon Dijon mustard

1 teaspoon minced garlic

1 teaspoon freshly squeezed lemon juice

¼ teaspoon kosher salt, plus more to taste

¾ cup olive oil

Freshly ground black pepper, to taste

1 teaspoon honey (optional)

Ground cayenne pepper (optional)

## FOR SERVING

½ cup microgreens or finely chopped Italian parsley, for garnish

## TIPS FOR SUCCESS

*Cook your sturgeon perfectly by using a meat thermometer inserted into the thickest part of the fish toward the end of grilling. Look for 150°F to 160°F, depending on preferred doneness.*

**Dry Salt Brine**  Massage the sturgeon with ¼ cup of the olive oil then a salt rub, using about 3 tablespoons kosher salt. Season with black pepper, wrap tightly in plastic wrap, and refrigerate for 2 hours. The dry brine can technically be skipped, but the flavor it adds is well worth the extra step. *Special Note: If not dry brining, upon removing from the refrigerator, brush the sturgeon liberally with about 1/4 cup olive oil, rub with about 2 teaspoons salt, and season generously with black pepper.*

**Bring to Room Temperature**  Let the sturgeon come to room temperature for 30 to 45 minutes before grilling. If brined, rinse off the excess salt, then pat dry with a paper towel. Brush the fish with the remaining 2 tablespoons of olive oil and sprinkle all sides with salt and pepper.

**Grill the Sturgeon**  Preheat the grill to 350°F to 375°F or medium-high heat. (You want to sear the fish and see grill marks.) Place the sturgeon on the grill, *skin side up*. The total time to grill will depend on the thickness of the fillet and the heat of your grill. Split grill time evenly, turning the fish as needed to grill on all sides. Plan on about 18 to 25 minutes for 3 pounds and 30 to 35 minutes for 4 pounds, and cook until the internal temperature reaches 150°F to 160°F.

**Grill the Oranges**  Brush the orange slices with olive oil and place on the grill about 10 minutes before the sturgeon is done, flipping after about 5 minutes. Remove once grill marks appear.

**Make the Citrus Vinaigrette**  While the fish grills, make the vinaigrette. Place the egg yolk, orange juice, apple cider vinegar, orange zest, lemon zest, mustard, garlic, lemon juice, and salt in a blender and blend on low for a few seconds to combine.

With the blender running, add the olive oil in a continuous, very slow stream until combined. You should have a nice smooth emulsion when finished.

(Alternatively, place the egg yolk, orange juice, apple cider vinegar, orange zest, lemon zest, mustard, garlic, lemon juice, and salt in a tall container and use an immersion blender to combine. Add the olive oil in a continuous, very slow stream until combined.)

Season to taste with salt and pepper. Stir in the honey (if using) to add sweetness or a dash of cayenne (if using) for a kick. Set aside until ready to plate.

**Let's Eat!**  Remove the sturgeon from the grill and let rest 5 to 10 minutes before transferring to a serving platter. Drizzle the fish generously with the orange citrus vinaigrette, place the grilled orange slices in a line across the top of the fillet, and sprinkle with the microgreens.

# Gung-ho for Gumbo

DAVID AND I discovered the **Red Arrow Roadhouse** about a month into our Harbor Country adventure. It's hard not to love the cozy, campy atmosphere, which has enough cabin kitsch to ensure you notice something new on every visit. The kiddo-friendly restaurant hums with warm energy as families and friends gather over generous plates ranging from the famous broasted chicken and epic ribs to homemade enchiladas and Roadhouse mudd pie!

On our first visit, I ordered the Lake Superior whitefish and David chose the Red Arrow Roadhouse gumbo. Both entrées came with salads, and the homemade dressings were so craveable, we wanted to buy bottles to go. We drove home satiated and smiling from the scrumptious meal and genuinely friendly service. Since day one, David has ordered the gumbo 100 percent of the time, and he was one happy gumbo guy when the Roadhouse kindly agreed to share the recipe. Also, a big thanks to the always fashion-forward Travis for always accommodating our random requests and making time for a quick chat no matter how busy he is!

## ★ Red Arrow Roadhouse

15710 Red Arrow Hwy. | Union Pier, MI

Red Arrow Roadhouse has become the place we go when we don't want to cook but don't really want to go out. It's comfortable, like eating at the home of a friend who always serves up a good time and hearty food that feeds the soul.

# Red Arrow Roadhouse Gumbo

**🍴 12–15** satisfying servings    🕐 **1 hr 30 min** active time    ⧖ **2 hrs** start to finish      Contributed by Chef Tim Hammerquist, Red Arrow Roadhouse

BACON ROUX

1 cup all-purpose flour

8 ounces bacon (to make
½ cup bacon grease)

GUMBO

4 pounds chicken breast,
cut into 1-inch cubes

Cajun spice blend (Chef Tim
uses Chef Paul Prudhomme.)

2 pounds precooked Andouille
sausage, sliced into 1-inch pieces
(Chef Tim uses Johnsonville.)

4 cups chopped white onions

3 cups chopped green, red,
or yellow bell peppers

2 cups chopped celery

4 tablespoons minced garlic

1 tablespoon dried basil

1 tablespoon dried thyme

2 bay leaves

6 cups chicken stock

4 cups beef stock

1 ounce hot sauce (Chef Tim
uses Frank's RedHot.)

1 ounce Worcestershire sauce

1 pound frozen okra, in pieces

SHRIMP (OPTIONAL BUT
AWESOME)

1½ pounds large shrimp,
peeled, cleaned, tails removed,
and defrosted if needed

Kosher salt, to taste

⅓ cup chicken stock

FOR SERVING

5 cups cooked white rice, or
4 cups cooked brown rice

**Brown the Flour** Preheat the oven to 350°F. Spread the flour in an even layer on a baking sheet and bake for about 30 minutes, or until lightly browned. Remove from the oven and set aside.

**Cook the Bacon** Raise the oven temperature to 425°F. Line a baking sheet with aluminum foil. Place the bacon strips on the baking sheet in a single layer and bake for about 20 minutes. Remove from the oven and, while still hot, pour the delicious golden bacon grease into a small bowl and set aside. You don't need the bacon itself for the recipe, so feel free to snack on it while making the gumbo, or wrap it up and refrigerate for another use.

**Make the Bacon Roux** In a medium pan or skillet, heat ½ cup of the bacon grease over medium heat for about 2 minutes. Sprinkle the toasted flour into the pan and whisk constantly to break up any lumps until the roux is smooth. Continue to cook over low heat, about 30 minutes, whisking often until the roux develops a deep brown color and rich, toasted flavor. Once done, remove from the heat and set aside.

**Make the Gumbo** Sprinkle the chicken with the Cajun spice blend. In a large stockpot over medium heat, *using no oil*, cook the chicken and sausage together until brown, about 10 minutes. Add the onions, peppers, celery, garlic, basil, thyme, and bay leaves and mix well to combine. After 5 minutes, add the chicken and beef stocks, hot sauce, and Worcestershire sauce and stir to combine. Bring to a boil. Add the bacon roux to the gumbo to thicken, whisking until fully combined. Add the okra, then stir and simmer for 15 to 20 minutes.

**Sauté the Shrimp (If Using)** At the Red Arrow Roadhouse, plump shrimp are perfectly cooked to order and added to each bowl of gumbo. If you plan on serving your gumbo with shrimp, which I totally support, heat a large pan over medium-high heat with a few tablespoons cooking oil or leftover bacon grease. Sprinkle the shrimp lightly with salt, then sauté for about 3 minutes per side, or just until firm and pink, deglazing the pan with the chicken stock at the end, before adding to the gumbo.

*Special Note: 1½ pounds of large shrimp is the amount to cook for this entire recipe and allows for about 3 shrimp per bowl. If not serving all the gumbo at once, just cook enough shrimp for each bowl you plan to serve. Gumbo without shrimp can be refrigerated in an airtight container for up to 3 days and only gets more delicious!*

**Let's Eat!** Chef Tim recommends serving the gumbo over rice, and my "gumbo guy" David agrees. If you want the genuine Roadhouse Gumbo experience, you'll just need to pay them a visit. At the restaurant, it's served over house-made Mexican rice and, yes, it's a game changer!

# So Here's the Dill

WE WALKED INTO the Great Lakes Surf & Turf event at Flagship Specialty Foods and Fish Market eager to try grilled sturgeon fish for the first time and experience a Mangalitsa hog roast! After filling our plates, we grabbed two seats in front of the live music and relaxed into an easy breezy Sunday.

When the band was done playing, a jovial gent took the stage with a broad smile, a glint in his eye, and a guitar in his hand. "One meatball!" he belted in a low, raspy voice. "One meatball! Well, you gets no bread with one meatball!" Over the next half hour, we were treated to a few more of this mystery musician's wonderfully quirky songs, and it was clear this guy would be fun to know!

Leaving the festivities, we stopped the "meatball musician" to praise his performance and introduce ourselves. We learned his name was Ron Spears, husband of Marge Spears, a darling pixie of a woman who was both vibrant and serene. Within 10 minutes of talking we learned they were avid tandem cyclists, wine aficionados, and consummate home chefs who had also mastered the arts of canning and pickling. We left the event both impressed and inspired by Ron, Marge, and the community of wonderfully interesting people we'd just met.

A few months later, we found ourselves at the Spearses' lovely abode for a paella feast. The dinner began with a crisp glass of champagne and a variety of pickled vegetables from their own garden. This cookbook wouldn't be complete without a pickling recipe, and who better to teach us all how to make perfectly pickled dilly beans and bread-and-butters than the Spearses themselves!

# Marge Spears's Perfectly Pickled Dilly Green Beans

🍴 **4** dilly-licious quarts   ⏳ **2 hrs** start to finish, plus 2 weeks to pickle                    Contributed by Marge Spears

## SPECIAL ITEMS NEEDED

Basic canner set, including a 21½-quart water bath canner pot, jar rack, jar funnel, jar lifter, magnetic lid lifter, and bubble remover. (You can get these kits at most local hardware stores or online. A water bath canner is a large pot with a jar rack that fits the bottom and a lid. You can find kits for $30 to $50, depending on what's included.)

4 (1-quart) mason jars with new lids and rings

---

4 pounds fresh green beans, rinsed, stemmed, and cut into jar-length pieces, if necessary (Most will not need trimming, which makes this go pretty quickly.)

4 cloves garlic

4 sprigs fresh dill

5 cups white vinegar (Make sure it's 5 percent.)

5 cups water

½ cup coarse kosher salt

## TIPS FOR SUCCESS
*Use a clean butter knife or long skewer to remove air bubbles from the jars before sealing. Insert gently into the jar a few times around the edges and in the center. Wipe the rims with a clean paper towel as needed. These two steps will reduce the chances of bacteria growing in your jars.*

## TIPS FOR SUCCESS
*Wait! What's "fingertip tight"? If you're planning to pickle and can, this is a term you'll want to know. It means to tighten the ring enough but not too much, just using the strength of your fingertips. No need to get those super strong biceps involved.*

*After about 24 hours, you can check that the lids are properly sealed by pressing in the center of the lid. When sealed correctly, the center should not flex up and down. If it does, refrigerate that jar and eat within a few days' time. All the jars should be refrigerated once opened.*

**Heat and Sterilize the Jars**  The jars should be sterilized prior to filling. There are two convenient ways to do this:

Option #1: Sterilize the jars by running them through the dishwasher, and then leave them in the closed dishwasher, open side down, until you are ready to fill them.

Option #2: Place the empty jars, without lids, right side up on the rack of a boiling water canner. Fill the canner and jars with hot (not boiling) water to cover the jars, about 1 inch above the tops of the jars. Bring to a boil and then continue to boil for 1 to 2 minutes. Carefully remove the jars and drain them one at a time, placing them open side down on a clean towel. You can save the hot water for processing your filled jars.

**Pack the Jars**  Bring a canner pot of water to a boil while you pack the jars. Pack the beans lengthwise in the clean, sterile jars, leaving ¼ inch of headroom from the tops of the jars. Stuff 1 clove garlic and 1 sprig dill into the middle of each jar. Pack all the jars at one time and lay the jars on their sides once packed, prior to adding liquid, to keep as sterile as possible.

**Make the Pickling Liquid**  In a large pot over high heat, bring the vinegar, water, and salt to a boil, stirring as needed, until the salt is dissolved. Ladle the vinegar mixture over the beans, leaving ¼ inch of headroom from the tops of the jars. Insert a clean butter knife into the jars as needed to remove any air bubbles, and wipe the rims with a clean paper towel as needed.

**Seal and Process**  Seal the jars using *new* lids and tighten the metal rings to be "fingertip tight," then place the sealed jars back into the canner rack and process for 15 minutes in a boiling water bath. Remove the jars and let cool at room temperature. Avoid crowding the jars together on your kitchen counter, giving them some space in between to facilitate cooling.

**Store and Wait Patiently**  Let the jars remain sealed for at least 2 weeks before opening. The dilly beans will be shelf-stable while properly sealed, but refrigerate after opening and enjoy within 1 month or so.

**Let's Eat!**  These are delicious served as part of a cheese and fruit platter or chopped up in a salad.

# Marge Spears's Bread-and-Butter Pickles

**¶1 6 pickle-licious quarts**   **⏱ 2 hrs** active time   **⧗ 10 hrs** start to finish, plus 2 weeks to pickle   Contributed by Marge Spears

SPECIAL ITEMS NEEDED

Basic canner set, including a 21½-quart water bath canner pot, jar rack, jar funnel, jar lifter, magnetic lid lifter, and bubble remover. (You can get these kits at most local hardware stores or online. A water bath canner is a large pot with a jar rack that fits the bottom and a lid. You can find kits for $30 to $50 depending on what's included.)

6 (1-quart) mason jars with new lids and rings

20 regular slicing cucumbers

4 medium yellow onions

½ cup coarse kosher salt

4 cups white vinegar (Make sure it's 5 percent.)

1 tablespoon dry mustard

2 teaspoons ground turmeric

3½ cups granulated sugar

**Prep and Salt the Cucumbers and Onions**  Wash the cucumbers, cut off the ends, and slice into rounds about ¼ inch thick. (Marge uses her Cuisinart food processor with the slicing blade attachment to do this work.)

Peel and thinly slice the onions, using the food processor if preferred. In a large pot or mixing bowl, combine the onions with the cucumbers and salt. Cover with a plate held down by a weight. (Marge uses a resealable plastic bag filled with water.) Let stand for 6 hours or overnight. The salt causes the cucumbers and onions to release a lot of water, hence the plate weight! Rinse and drain well, until the cucumbers no longer taste salty (probably three changes of water). Once this step is complete, sterilize your jars and make your pickling liquid.

**Heat and Sterilize the Jars**  The jars should be sterilized prior to filling. There are two convenient ways to do this:

Option #1: Sterilize the jars by running them through the dishwasher, and then leave them in the closed dishwasher, open side down, until you are ready to fill them.

Option #2: Place the empty jars, without lids, right side up on the rack of a boiling water canner. Fill the canner and jars with hot (not boiling) water to cover the jars, about 1 inch above the tops of the jars. Bring to a boil and then continue to boil for 1 to 2 minutes. Carefully remove the jars and drain them one at a time, placing them open side down on a clean towel. You can save the hot water for processing your filled jars.

**Make the Pickling Liquid**  Combine the vinegar, dry mustard, turmeric, and sugar in a large pot over medium-high heat and bring to a boil. Boil for 5 minutes, stirring as needed, until the sugar is dissolved. Add the rinsed cucumbers and onions and bring to a simmer. Don't boil, or the vegetables will become mushy. Stir periodically to ensure the mixture is heated through. Remove from the heat and promptly pack the jars.

**Pack the Jars, Seal, and Process**  Bring a canning pot of water to a boil while you pack the jars. Use tongs to fill each jar with as many cucumbers and onions as you can, then ladle in the liquid, leaving ½ inch of headroom from the tops of the jars. *Pack all the jars at one time.* Insert a clean butter knife into the jars as needed to remove any air bubbles, and wipe the rims with a clean paper towel as needed. Seal the jars using *new* lids and tighten the metal rings to be "fingertip tight," then place the sealed jars back into the canner rack and process for 10 minutes in a boiling water bath. Remove the jars and let cool at room temperature.

**Store and Wait Patiently**  Let the jars remain sealed for at least 2 weeks before opening. The pickles will be shelf-stable while properly sealed, but refrigerate after opening and enjoy within 1 month or so.

**Let's Eat!**  These pickles are awesome alone, chopped in a salad, or served with your favorite sandwich. Now you can relish your pickles all year long!

# Class by the Glass

A LONG LIFE'S JOURNEY, there are some people who you immediately like. For me, Susan was one of those people. Wherever she goes, a trail of elegant fun follows. On weekends Susan would often escape from Chicago to her Michigan home in Harbor Country, which meant little to us, until it meant everything to us.

One day I finally asked Susan, "What do you do in Michigan, anyway?"

With a grin of contentment she said, "You read, nap, and cook. You go on walks and sleep in late." It wasn't what she said but how she said it that piqued my interest. This was the sound of happiness stemming from simple acts of relaxation. I wanted to feel that kind of happy.

One spring morning, when David awoke and wanted to drive to Michigan for the day, I recalled this conversation with Susan and quickly got on board.

Today we thank our dear friend for sharing her secret retreat, which is 90 minutes from Chicago but a world away. Those lucky enough to be hosted in her lovely abode, known as the Red Door Inn, are often treated to an RDI Manhattan or two, depending on the night.

# The RDI Manhattan

🍸 **1** perfect serving    ⧗ **5 min** start to finish      Contributed by Susan Szymanski

SPECIAL ITEMS NEEDED

Fabulous vintage cocktail glass

Ice

1 Luxardo cherry

2 ounces W. L. Weller bourbon

1 ounce Cocchi Storico
Vermouth di Torino

4 shakes Angostura Bitters

**Mix It Up** Fill a cocktail shaker with ice. Spoon the cherry into a cocktail glass with a long cocktail stirring spoon, then place the spoon in the cocktail shaker. Pour in the bourbon and vermouth, then shake in the bitters. Let the cocktail rest for 1 minute, then stir for 1 minute and strain into the cocktail glass.

**Let's Drink!** Sip and savor in great company. Always.

# Smooth Journey Ahead

THE WALLS OF THE **Journeyman Distillery** in Three Oaks, Michigan, hold a lot of history and whiskey! The first time we visited the distillery, the unmistakable scent of fermenting grain welcomed us. The massive bar beckons you to indulge in a perfect craft cocktails made with house-distilled spirits.

While the guest of honor at the party here is definitely whiskey, other classics, such as Red Arrow Vodka and Road's End Rum, can also be imbibed.

We can now celebrate the spirit of Harbor Country at home, Journeyman-style, with the whiskey-based E. K. Warren (page 220) and the always lovely Lavender Gimlet with Bilberry Black Hearts Gin (page 222), my favorite Journeyman spirit!

Behind the E. K. Warren cocktail: in the late 1800s, entrepreneur E. K. Warren developed a product made from the quill of a turkey feather called the Featherbone. The Featherbone product was used as a replacement for the whalebone found in women's corsets and was used to manufacture over 100 different kinds of buggy whips. Warren took his product worldwide, amassing a fortune.

Warren was also a staunch prohibitionist. Today, Journeyman Distillery resides in the Featherbone Factory building and proudly tells the story of E. K. Warren. If he were around today, he might not sidle up to the bar for a drink, given his prohibitionist past, but he would surely toast to good old-fashioned manufacturing and to the endeavor of entrepreneurship. Cheers to E. K. and his lasting legacy!

★ Journeyman Distillery and Staymaker Restaurant

109 Generations Dr. | Three Oaks, MI

★ The Acorn Theater

107 Generation Dr. | Three Oaks, MI

One of our favorite Saturday night traditions is getting dinner and drinks at Journeyman's Staymaker Restaurant , followed by a show at The Acorn Theater.

# Journeyman Distillery E. K. Warren

🍸 **1** unforgettable serving  ⏳ **5 min** start to finish                    Contributed by Journeyman Distillery

1½ ounces Journeyman Last Feather Rye Whiskey

½ ounce simple syrup

½ ounce freshly squeezed lemon juice

2 dashes Angostura Bitters

Ice

1 lemon peel, for garnish

1 Luxardo cherry, for garnish

**Mix It Up** In a cocktail shaker, stir the whiskey, simple syrup, lemon juice, and bitters with ice. Strain into a rocks glass over ice. Garnish with the lemon peel and cherry.

**Let's Drink!** Savor every sip.

# Journeyman Distillery Lavender Gimlet

🍸 **1** summer-loving serving   🕐 **10 min** active time   ⏳ **4 hrs 10 min** start to finish

Contributed by  Journeyman Distillery

### LAVENDER-INFUSED GIN

1 teaspoon dried lavender buds

1 cup Journeyman Bilberry
Black Hearts Gin

### LAVENDER GIMLET COCKTAIL

Ice

2 ounces lavender-infused
Journeyman Bilberry
Black Hearts Gin

½ ounce freshly squeezed
grapefruit juice

½ ounce freshly
squeezed lime juice

½ ounce simple syrup

### TIPS FOR SUCCESS

*Make 2 and toast with a friend.*

*Lavender can be a strong-tasting ingredient. You may want to start the infusion process using a smaller amount and adjust to taste. You can always add more lavender or gin.*

**Infuse**  In a mason jar, steep the dried lavender buds in the Bilberry Black Hearts Gin for a minimum of 4 hours. You can strain out the lavender or leave it in, whatever your pleasure, and store the gin in the mason jar in the refrigerator until ready to enjoy. This will make enough infused gin for 4 gimlets.

**Mix It Up**  In a cocktail shaker with ice, shake the gin, grapefruit juice, lime juice, and simple syrup. Pour into a coupe glass.

**Let's Drink!**  Sip and smile.

# My Harbor Country Favorites

## Arts

**The Acorn Theater**
107 Generation Dr.
Three Oaks, MI 49128
269-756-3879
www.acornlive.org

**Joe Hindley Studio Gallery**
5861 Sawyer Rd.
Sawyer, MI 49125
269-426-8516
www.hindleyfineart.org

**School of American Music**
3 N. Elm St.
Three Oaks, MI 49128
269-409-1191
www.schoolofamericanmusic.com

## Beaches

**Cherry Beach**
13897 S. Cherry Beach
Harbert, MI 49128

**Townline Beach**
10379 Townline Rd.
Union Pier, MI 49129

**Warren Dunes State Park**
12032 Red Arrow Hwy.
Sawyer, MI 49125
269-426-4013

## Breweries, Wineries, Distilleries, and Coffee Shops

**Greenbush Brewing Co.**
5885 Sawyer Rd.
Sawyer, MI 49125
269-405-1076
www.greenbushbrewing.com

**Infusco Coffee Roasters**
5846 Sawyer Rd.
Sawyer, MI 49125
269-213-5282
www.infuscocoffee.com

**Journeyman Distillery**
109 Generations Dr.
Three Oaks, MI 49128
269-820-2050
www.journeymandistillery.com

**Lemon Creek Winery and Farm Market**
533 E. Lemon Creek Rd.
Berrien Springs, MI 49103
269-471-1321
www.lemoncreekwinery.com

**Round Barn Tasting Room**
9185 Union Pier Rd.
Union Pier, MI 49129
269-469-6885
www.roundbarn.com

**St. Julian Winery Tasting Room**
9145 Union Pier Rd.
Union Pier, MI 49129
269-469-3150
www.stjulian.com

**Tabor Hill Winery and Restaurant**
185 Mt. Tabor Rd.
Buchanan, MI 49107
269-422-1161
www.taborhill.com

## Events

**Apple Cider Century**
888-877-2068
www.applecidercentury.com
Annually in September

## Farms, U-pick Produce, and Other Food Vendors

**Billy Boy's Blueberry Barn**
650 Freyer Rd.
Michigan City, IN 46360
219-872-7477
www.billyboysblueberrybarn.com

**The Blueberry Patch**
7015 Blackwell Dr.
Sawyer, MI 49125
269-426-4521

**Dinges' Fall Harvest**
15219 Mill Rd.
Three Oaks, MI 49128
269-426-4034

**Fruitbelt**
269-743-6535
www.fruitbelt.com

**Garwood Orchards**
5911 W. 50 S
La Porte, IN 46350
219-362-4385

**Granor Farm**
3480 Warren Woods Rd.
Three Oaks, MI 49128
www.granorfarm.com

**Hansing's Happy Hens**
574-310-0717

**Kaminski Farms**
16682 S. Schwark Rd.
Three Oaks, MI 49128
269-756-7457
www.kaminskifarms.com

**Lehman's Orchard**
2280 Portage Rd.
Niles, MI 49120
269-683-9078
www.lehmansorchard.com

**Nye Heritage Farms and Apple Barn**
3151 Niles Rd.
St. Joseph, MI 49085
269-429-0596
www.nyesapplebarn.com

**Red Arrow Roasters**
269-220-0545
www.redarrowroasters.com

**Springhope Farm**
18720 Cleveland Ave.
Galien, MI 49113
269-545-8313
www.springhopefarm.com

**Twin Maple Orchards**
15352 Cleveland Ave.
Galien, MI 49113
269-545-8840
www.twinmapleorchards.com

## Fireworks Stores

**Black Bull Fireworks**
10505 US-12
Michigan City, IN 46360
219-861-0980
www.blackbullfireworks.com

**Krazy Kaplans Fireworks**
1433 Indianapolis Blvd.
Whiting, IN 46394
219-473-0511

## Gift and Home Decor Shops

**Customs Imports**
139 N. Whittaker St.
New Buffalo, MI 49117
269-469-9180
www.customsimports.com

**Hearthwoods Custom Furnishings**
15310 Red Arrow Hwy.
Lakeside, MI 49116
269-469-5551
www.hearthwoods.com

**Lake Interiors**
15412 Red Arrow Hwy.
Lakeside, MI 49116
269-231-5434
www.lakeinteriorsinc.com

**Perennial Accents**
220 State St.
St. Joseph, MI 49085
269-983-5791
www.perennialaccents.com

**Sawyer Home and Garden Center**
5865 Sawyer Rd.
Sawyer, MI 49125
269-426-8810
www.sawyergardencenter.com

**Sojourn**
12908 Red Arrow Hwy.
Sawyer, MI 49125
269-426-4247
www.sojournastore.com

**The Villager**
100 N. Whittaker St.
New Buffalo, MI 49117
269-469-6151

## Hotels

**The Harbor Grand Hotel**
111 W. Water St.
New Buffalo, MI 49117
888-605-6800
www.harborgrand.com

**Marina Grand Resort**
600 W. Water St.
New Buffalo, MI 49117
877-945-8600
www.marinagrandresort.com

## Markets and Specialty Food Stores

**Barney's Market**
10 N. Thompson St.
New Buffalo, MI 49117
269-469-1210
www.barneysnb.com

**Flagship Specialty Foods and Fish Market**
14939 Red Arrow Hwy.
Lakeside, MI 49116
269-231-5432
www.flagship-foods.com

**New Buffalo Farmers Market**
910 W. Buffalo St.
New Buffalo, MI 49117
312-965-9114
www.newbuffalofarmersmarket.com

**Skip's New Buffalo European Farmers Market**
16710 Lakeshore Rd.
New Buffalo, MI 49117
269-469-3341

**Whistle Stop Grocery**
15700 Red Arrow Hwy.
Union Pier, MI 49129
269-469-6700
www.whistlestopgrocery.com

**Sawyer Home and Garden Center**
5865 Sawyer Rd.
Sawyer, MI 49125
269-426-8810
www.sawyergardencenter.com

## Restaurants and Bakeries

**Bentwood Tavern**
600 W. Water St.
New Buffalo, MI 49117
269-469-1699
www.bentwoodtavern.com

**Black Currant Bakehouse**
9911 Town Line Ave.
Union Pier, MI 49129
269-586-3830
www.blackcurrantbakehouse.com

**David's Delicatessen**
30 N. Whittaker St.
New Buffalo, MI 49117
269-469-7177
www.davidsdeliandcoffee.com

**Froehlich's Kitchen and Pantry**
19 N. Elm St.
Three Oaks, MI 49128
269-756-6002
www.shopfroehlichs.com

**Greenbush Brewing Co.**
5885 Sawyer Rd.
Sawyer, MI 49125
269-405-1076
www.greenbushbrewing.com

**Houndstooth Restaurant**
132 Pipestone St.
Benton Harbor, MI 49022
269-252-5250
www.eathoundstooth.com

**Luisa's Café and Harbert Swedish Bakery**
13698 Red Arrow Hwy.
Harbert, MI 49115
269-469-9037
www.luisascafe.com

**The Peasant's Pantry**
12856 Red Arrow Hwy.
Sawyer, MI 49125
269-405-1284
www.thepeasantspantry.com

**Red Arrow Roadhouse**
15710 Red Arrow Hwy.
Union Pier, MI 49129
269-469-3939
www.redarrowroadhouse.com

**Skip's Restaurant**
16710 Lakeshore Rd.
New Buffalo, MI 49117
269-469-3341
www.skipsrestaurantandcatering.com

**Staymaker Restaurant**
109 Generations Dr.
Three Oaks, MI 49128
269-820-2050
www.journeymandistillery.com
/staymaker

**The Stray Dog Bar & Grill**
245 N. Whittaker St.
New Buffalo, MI 49117
269-469-2727
www.thestraydog.com

**Terrace Room**
111 W. Water St.
New Buffalo, MI 49117
269-469-7950
www.terraceroomhg.com

**Whistle Stop Grocery**
15700 Red Arrow Hwy.
Union Pier, MI 49129
269-469-6700
www.whistlestopgrocery.com

# Acknowledgments

T o  t h e  m i c r o v i l l a g e  of gracious people who helped make this cookbook dream a reality, my gratitude is vast. Because I believe freshly baked goods are worth 1,000 words, let it be known to all who supported me on this journey that I owe you several batches of homemade cookies and a cup of locally roasted coffee.

I'd like to extend a massive, frosting-coated, sprinkle-covered thank-you to:

My exceptional photographer, **Gabrielle Sukich**, who went above and beyond from the day we decided to jump down this rabbit hole together. Thank you for shooting with your heart, for your endless patience, and for doing whatever it took to get the shot . . . including wading into a freezing Lake Michigan in April, in jeans, to position my paddleboard with one hand while shooting photos with the other! To me you will always be "Gabrielle the Great!"

The team at **Agate Publishing**, including president and founder **Doug Seibold**, associate managing editor **Helena Hunt**, designer **Morgan Krehbiel**, proofreader **Jessica Easto**, and associate manager of publicity **Jacqueline Jarik**. Thank you all for sharing your talents to help transform my vision into something even better. I truly appreciate your patience, willingness to collaborate, and the time spent bringing *Hungry for Harbor Country* to a wider audience.

**Jennifer Solheim**, editorial consultant, who patiently guided me through the adventure of being a first-time author. This book is a far more delicious read thanks to your deft editing skills.

**David Navama**, husband, ultimate book designer, project manager, taste tester, and best friend. Your endless patience (even at 4 a.m.), strong guidance, and ability to move mountains most would perceive as immovable are what allowed me to cross the finish line.

**Laura and Fred Jolly**, our New Buffalo besties. Thank you for taking us under your wings and making us feel at home in Harbor Country.

**The beloved local eateries and friends** for graciously contributing "secret local recipes" so we can all make some of Harbor Country's finest food at home: Bentwood Tavern, David's Delicatessen, Flagship Specialty Foods and Fish Market, Luisa's Café and Harbert Swedish Bakery, Red Arrow Roadhouse, Journeyman Distillery, Terrace Room, Whistle Stop Grocery, Marge and Ron Spears, and Susan Szymanski.

**The coffee shops** that kept me caffeinated and gave me a place to write this book in the perfect semisolitude that only a café with free Wi-Fi can provide: David's Delicatessen (New

Buffalo) and Emma, Joe, Stacey, and team for fueling me with oat milk au laits and mugs of phenomenal vegan chili. Dollop (Chicago) for opening early and closing late. Infusco Coffee Roasters (Sawyer) and Aaron, Nick, Stefani, David, Eric, and team for weighing in on a variety of recipes and photos. A special thanks to Nick for connecting me with Gabrielle when I needed to find a local food photographer. Wildberry Pancakes and Café (Chicago) for fueling my drives to Michigan with great coffee.

**Barney's Market** and **Sawyer Home and Garden Center** for the incredible selection of ingredients available at both fine markets, from gluten-free flours, chia seeds, and dried figs to duck eggs, local cherry wine, and fresh Michigan produce. It's because of these stores that I was able to shop locally to test all my recipes!

**My family-in-law, Rosanne, Shlomo, Jack, Daniel, Talia,** and **Eileen.** Thank you for offering to test recipes, always encouraging me to follow my foodie dreams, and sharing your delicious Shabbat dinners with me on many a Friday night!

**My forever friends for your endless support always:** Dan and Kathy Jones; Tiffany and Garrett Banks; Erica Silverstein; Julie and Kevin Williams; Jenny and Nick Semaca; Julie Bonicelli and Luis Galindo; Izabel, Bella, Gabe, and Tony Olson and family; Lara, Jay, and Jack; Amy Zwikel; Sigi-Blu and Jesse Kouffman; Erin Burkhardt and Dalton Grant; Claire and Kyle Volenik; Stephanie and Bart Webster; Steffi, Luca, Nico, and Mike Neth; Dana and Jarred Walker; Sean Stoner; Mike Misrachi; DJ Paul; Kim De Jesus; and Leslie Bradshaw.

**House hunters:** Margaret Baczkowski, our incredible Chicago realtor, who introduced us to the amazing Michigan realtors Liz Roch and Mary Lynn Kormanik. Without the three of you, we wouldn't have found Camp Navama!

**The many other hands and hearts that contributed to the creation of this book in so many different ways:** Chef Alberto Ilescas, Ali Valvo, Anna Alexopoulos, Ava Galbraith, Brooke Nyman, Caroline Ramsay, Carrol and Bob Farley, Chelsey Erickson, Cynthia Berkshire, Dan Kluko, food stylist Emily Anstadt, Emily Berkshire, Chef Eva Frahm, Harbor Country Chamber of Commerce, Chef James Galbraith, Jennifer and Chef Tim Trout, Chef Jenny Drilon, Jessica Nance, Katie Carpenter and *Edible Michiana* magazine, Chef Kelsey Morgan, Lee and Elaine Dinges and Dinges' Fall Harvest, Luisa Mills, Milan Kluko, Paddy Lauber and Kerry Shintani, Chef Rachel Collins and Flagship team, Chef Robert Lesniewski, Robert Kemper, Robert Shearer, Sharon and Pat O'Hara, Stephanie Mahan, Sturgeon Beach community, Chef Tim Hammerquist, Tom Jolly, Travis Worden, and Vivian May.

# Index

# Shared Memorable Meals

When our first Harbor Country autumn arrived, we looked back at summer wishing we'd kept a guest book detailing the memories made and meals shared with many of our nearest and dearest. Here is a space to record some of your family's most magical moments.

DATE                    GUESTS                          MEMORABLE MEAL

_____          _____          _____

_____          _____          _____

_____          _____          _____

_____          _____          _____

_____          _____          _____

_____          _____          _____

_____          _____          _____

_____          _____          _____

_____          _____          _____

_____          _____          _____

# About the Author

**Lindsay Navama** is a recipe developer, natural foods expert specializing in gluten- and dairy-free products, writer, and culinary content creator. She's the friend you call when you want a craveable cookie recipe, need to know what to do with watermelon radishes, or are looking for a recommendation for the best foaming almond milk.

Born in Lake Tahoe to a food-loving family, she developed her passion for all things culinary at an early age. After earning a degree in broadcast journalism from Arizona State University, she moved to Los Angeles to pursue careers in both acting and food, but her love for baking won. She opened Cookies Couture, a boutique bakery that helped customers design the cookies of their wildest dreams. While living in L.A., Lindsay appeared as the resident chef on Simon Fuller's *If I Can Dream* and on KTLA news as a food personality, and she was a host on Plum TV.

Her (now) husband David's gluten and dairy sensitivities inspired her to create "secretly" allergy-friendly recipes craveable enough for *everyone* to enjoy. With Lindsay's passion for discovering the best natural foods on the market, she became director of sales for Destini, a technology company David founded to help all people easily find specific food and beverage products, both locally and online.

Stop by ThirdCoastKitchen.com to discover Lindsay's newest recipes, videos, favorite products, and ongoing tales from her Harbor Country and Chicago kitchens. She splits her time between Illinois and Michigan with David and their daughter, Stella.